WORK AFTER WORK

To RJH
For your Retirement

WORK AFTER WORK

Judy Kirby

Foreword by
The Hon Greville Janner

Quiller Press
London

First published 1984 by Quiller Press Ltd
50 Albemarle Street, London W1X 4BD
Copyright © 1984 Retired Executives Action Clearing House.

ISBN 0 907621 27 9

All rights reserved. No part of this book may be reproduced or transmitted, in any form or by any means, without permission of the publishers

Design and production in association with
Book Production Consultants, 47 Norfolk Street, Cambridge.

Printed by Richard Clay (The Chaucer Press) Limited, Bungay, Suffolk

Contents

Foreword by the Hon Greville Janner, QC, MP	7
1. The White Economy and Retirement Retirement: another word for unemployment?	9
2. The Voluntary Sector How it began — what *is* a charity? — Not a one-way deal	19
3. Industry: Coming in Out of the Cold May we borrow your accountant? — Secondment's impact on society — Putting secondment into perspective	37
4. Getting the Job What are the jobs? — Who are the people? — In the market place — Read all about it! — Volunteer bureaux	52
5. So You Still Want Money? Are there other ways of earning after retirement?	70
6. Top Ten Profiles of ten leading grant-seeking charities	80
7. On a Jet Plane Voluntary Service Overseas — British Executive Service Overseas	113
8. In the Country	121
9. Who's Afraid of Fund Raising?	126
Appendix A Classified Index of Voluntary Groups in the United Kingdom	130
Appendix B Index of Established Enterprise Agencies	143
Appendix C Index of Organisations for Whose Retired Executives REACH has Secured Suitable Matches	154
Index	155

ACKNOWLEDGEMENT

I would like to thank everyone who supplied me with facts, figures and opinions for this book. All the profiles, except for Bill Evans, were taken from REACH's records. Particular thanks to the National Council for Voluntary Organisations for permission to reprint the classified list of voluntary groups. The full directory can be bought from NCVO, 26 Bedford Square, London, WC1 for £4.95.

REACH

Retired Executives Action Clearing House (REACH) acts as a link to bring retired executives from business and industry to work on an expenses-only basis for charities, voluntary organisations and community groups which need but cannot afford their specialist skills.

FOREWORD

The Hon Greville Janner, QC, MP
President of REACH

We British are well balanced — we have a chip on each shoulder. The first we get when we are young and leave school or university and cannot get work, possibly because someone who wishes to retire is unable to do so because of our crazy pension arrangements. The other arrives at the far end of the age range when we wish to retire but are forced to soldier on, perhaps because, again, our pension is related to our final year's earnings — or (and here is where REACH is more likely to be of help) because we are required to retire when we have much to give and nothing to fear except boredom. A combination of 'early redundancy' and 'late retirement' produces the sort of madness which can only build our human scrap heap.

REACH is aimed at the fit and fearless — those who have been retired, voluntarily or compulsorily, but who are ready, anxious, willing and able to serve, and most unready to lie down and die. REACH is for those who wish to give service, aimed at the benefit of those who receive it, but which, of course, helps the giver too.

A bank manager recently told me that a survey in his organisation revealed that managers who take on no other work when they retire usually die within about eighteen months. The loss is not only that of their families, but of the community.

So we must learn to train people to make good use of the years after they have given up active business life. No one should need to fade away and expire.

I met Morarji Desai, Prime Minister of India at the age of eighty-three. That was four years ago: last year, I found him on the political campaign trail in South India, happily at work.

My father went to his solicitor's office and to the House of Lords until he was eighty-seven. He used to joke that he only did so to keep

Work After Work

his son. But in fact the work kept him alive and happy. Much of his best contributions to society were made after he reached the age of seventy-five.

So I salute this valuable book, with its unique, serious and detailed scrutiny of the ways in which retired people can discover how to make their experience useful to the communities in which they live. It should also help voluntary organisations keen to find skilled and experienced help for those whom they serve.

I commend both the book and the work of REACH, first to industry and commerce. They are examples of fine public spirit, combined with private and enlightened self-interest.

Second, the book is for retired executives themselves. It points the trail to a new purpose in an extended and enjoyable life of service, with new reasons for getting up in the morning.

Finally, to those of us who are not yet retired, the book brings a reassurance that we shall still be needed. Not all of us will be able to be prime ministers or professional consultants in our eighties, but at least this book helps us to reach out towards old age in the knowledge that our strivings and usefulness will not end with retirement.

'Ah, but man's reach should exceed his grasp, or what's a heaven for?' This book increases our reach — and the prospect of retaining a measure of heaven on earth. Even if we do not know where we will be going hereafter, REACH — and this book — will help us to improve our prospects while we are here.

GREVILLE JANNER

CHAPTER ONE

THE WHITE ECONOMY AND RETIREMENT

What has a workforce of 3 million, putting in 18 million hours a week, and an income of £5,000 million?

You would be forgiven for thinking this is a multinational or a major nationalised industry, but you'd be wrong. This organisational giant resides in neither private nor public zone. It has been nicknamed 'the white economy'. It is the voluntary sector. What was affectionately and contemptuously called 'do-gooding' in the past has now become big business. There is a breathtaking diversity of enterprise spanning nearly 200,000 voluntary groups and the 'employees' number more than the total full-time workforce of the personal social services.

Even in the recession, money flows into the voluntary sector. People, companies and government donate millions of pounds yearly — one estimate puts it at £2,600 million. And the recession has brought with it a new and quite unforeseen role for the voluntary sector: that of running job creation and training schemes to help stem the tragedy of youth unemployment. This widely recognised new role conceals a range of changes which are not so readily understood. But they are important and significant particularly in the relationship between the voluntary sector and the rest of society.

The enormous shakeout of jobs in the economy has affected the young most publicly. But it has also had a profound effect on others who might be described as being in the margins of the labour force: older workers, women, the unskilled and semi-skilled, immigrants. They are the ones who have lost their jobs first and who have found new ones either difficult or impossible to find.

There are two public responses to this catastrophe. The first, and

Work After Work

largely unspoken one, is the natural inclination to blame the victim for his or her own troubles. It is still obvious that many people believe that unemployment only affects individuals who in some way bring it on themselves, either by failing to work hard enough, or to educate themselves properly, or to secure the right training and experience.

This can be difficult to reconcile with the fact that there are simply not enough jobs to go round. But many people are convinced that the best and most useful way to help unemployed people is to offer them training so that they can improve themselves.

The second response is the growth of a belief that the generation of new wealth and jobs will only take place in small businesses, through local efforts at development and perhaps as a result of unconventional ventures. A logical conclusion to this is that if the unemployed are going to play a part in the regeneration of wealth and employment, they must be offered training and education which will improve their ability to tackle a wide range of jobs and even, in many cases, put them in a position where they themselves can create new opportunities.

There are, no doubt, plenty of people who will argue fairly convincingly that the first of these attitudes is simply primitive, while the second is evidence of woolly and wishful thinking. But as a result of these two lines of thought a whole new approach to training has been devised and put in hand. This comes in response to the crisis of unemployment and to the collapsing British system of training in industry, which has been based upon time-serving and the acquisition of skills. And it amounts to nothing less than a revolution in British training practice. The most significant aspect of this great change is that training for young people is now being based far more on the development of ability, leading to the acquisition of skills, and is therefore educational in much of its method. The thinking behind this approach is that in a job market which is at best uncertain, demands for skills will change substantially over time, and all workers will need to update their skills through retraining during their working lives.

The flexible worker will be capable of transferring 'core' skills and abilities from the demands of one job or occupation to another and thus survive in work.

The White Economy and Retirement

Those who still want to see the continued existence of craftsmen and experts find this an unwelcome prospect because it will produce people with a range of skills and abilities, rather than specialists who have been highly trained. This change of view of what training ought to be about has opened the door to a whole range of people who would not previously have been thought of as industrial trainers. This has resulted in training taking place in settings which might, not so long ago, have been considered unlikely. Thus voluntary organisations, and even quite small community groups, have found themselves accepted by the Manpower Services Commission as viable trainers — especially of young people — sometimes offering training in work allied to the social services. Just as often they find themselves setting up small workshops offering training through the production of goods or services by fairly conventional industrial methods.

Local authorities have also either encouraged or even taken on this kind of sponsorship themselves and have increasingly tended to see the whole exercise as part of their legitimate efforts to regenerate their local economies. It has been quite feasible for a training workshop run under the Youth Opportunities Programme, or latterly under the Youth Training Scheme, to have an annual throughput of 50 trainees, to provide employment for eight or nine adult staff and to have a total cash turnover of something close to £200,000 a year. Whichever way you look at that, this constitutes a significant net contribution to a local economy where jobs may be disappearing and businesses are either becoming insolvent or at least pulling in their horns. Businessmen have increasingly begun to take all this seriously, not just as a means of providing training in sympathy with the uncertainty of the times, but also as a potentially influential means of stimulating, and on occasions developing, the manufacturing and trading base, for the formation of small enterprises.

Training has changed. Its significance is being re-evaluated. New people and new combinations of people are seeing training and preparation for work as their legitimate business. This new development has absorbed a lot of government money. The Youth Opportunities Programme has recently been receiving nearly £400 million annually and voluntary groups played an important part in the national and local economy managing sizeable training schemes.

Work After Work

Government measures to provide job opportunities during 1982–3 for sixteen-year-olds centre on the £950 million Youth Training Scheme which aims to provide 460,000 places in training schemes. During 1983 the Department of Health and Social Security had more than £7 million to spend on grants to organisations helping unemployed people take on voluntary work in the health and social services. The government had originally planned £3.3 million for this charity programme, but agreed to make more money available because many projects were already full up early in the year.

With budgets of these proportions you would expect that the management of voluntary enterprises needed to be every bit as creative and worldly as their commercial counterparts. Estates must be managed, chains of charity shops run professionally, training schemes administered, community centres built, investments handled expertly.

But what this vast empire lacks is expertise. Some financial and organisational wizards exist in it but they are rare. Problem solvers are sometimes seconded from industry, but what the empire needs are motivated men and women who are unhindered by the need to earn salaries, to take it forward into the high-tech, computerised eighties. Where can they be found? Well, the answer may lie in the fact that many more business and professional people are now finishing their careers earlier than they may have planned; in 1971 94 per cent of men aged between 45 and 64 were economically active. Ten years later the proportion was down to 88 per cent and in April 1982 half the men in the 60 to 64 age group on the unemployment register had been there for more than a year (*Social Trends* 13). Could it be that the future of the white economy lies amongst the swelling ranks of the retired?

DESMOND AINSBURY

Age 59

Previous occupation British Steel works manager at Workington and Barrow, responsible for 1,000 employees.

The White Economy and Retirement

Occupation now Helping young people find jobs in brass and aluminium foundry work, metal finishing and fabrication, silk screen printing, administration, building maintenance and catering.

Mr Ainsbury took early retirement at 55. After the nominal 'honeymoon' period he took the fourth job offered him by REACH, a placement officer with Workshop 6 in Sheffield where he and his wife had moved.

Workshop 6 has a relentless task — finding work for the fifty 16 to 19-year-olds who spend a year there learning a trade. In 1982 a third of the young people training found jobs. The city has 10,000 unemployed young people and Desmond Ainsbury has a tough time persuading potential employers to take some of them on.

He admits it is increasingly difficult to find vacancies. 'It is very much like throwing bread upon the waters,' he says, 'hoping of course that some return will come in not many days.'

Desmond Ainsbury (left) with his new 'team', the young people of Workshop 6. The Workshop manager is on the right. Picture by courtesy of the Sheffield Morning Telegraph.

Work After Work

Workshop 6 is mainly funded by the Manpower Services Commission. Mr Ainsbury was attracted to its work 'as an antidote to the scrapheap syndrome, primarily'.

But his commitment goes further than that. 'I feel I am discharging a debt. My generation, particularly those like myself in manufacture, are in no small measure responsible for the inefficiency and bad labour practices all too evident today.

'We let it happen. Maybe my efforts with Workshop 6 may wash out some of this blot.'

Retirement: another word for unemployment?

For a joyful appraisal of the values of maturity, you need look no further than Cicero. Modern gerontologists have, on the other hand, painted a desperate picture of a coming 'geriatric explosion'. We are assailed with the medical facts of ageing; what we can expect physically and mentally and how we can allay the worst with drugs and judicious living. But for Cicero age was a matter for pride: 'Your state was a great one; tell me, how did you lose it in so short a time?' he pointedly queries in *On Old Age and Friendship*. People with no inner resources for living the good and happy life found every age a burden, he believed. Everyone prayed to reach old age but when they did achieve it they promptly started to complain! 'You see,' he wrote, 'foolish and thoughtless men charge old age with weakness and faults that are really their own.'

Cicero would have been horrified at the apologetic tone of much present-day writing on retirement. Those who have spent a lifetime in decision-making are urged to switch their energy to planning creative leisure, almost as a compensation for the loss of work. You may not have fallen into the trap of workaholism in your career, but equally you were probably not addicted to leisure either. If you've always enjoyed free time — and there was certainly not enough of it during a busy career — you'll go on enjoying it. If you didn't, there's no reason to expect you'll suddenly start doing so just because you've quit paid work.

The White Economy and Retirement

Classically, and historically, retirement has been about leisure, which is strange in a society increasingly conscious of productivity and cost effectiveness. Can there be anything more wasteful than discarding valuable experience gained during a whole lifetime of work? And there is no tradition of older employees passing on their 'tricks of the trade' to those starting out, despite the undeniable fact that new technologies can never be the whole success story in any industry. Indeed, work itself is under scrutiny now and the debate over its organisation is heating up. Many people find it illogical that one section (the senior executives and professionals) of the population should be overworked while another section is bereft of work through unemployment, redundancy and retirement. It has been argued that there is not enough 'work' to go round in today's world, yet needs constantly increase. What is wanted is a different approach to work so that flexible patterns may eventually replace our former rigid structure. One example is maternity, and to a lesser extent paternity, leave — enabling parents to 'retire' temporarily and to return to work later. Recent legislation has not been without snags but it is furthering the concept of organising work more according to people's needs. Job splitting or sharing, even with its administrative problems, is another attempt in this direction.

The price for the western way of work is paid in retirement. For those whose jobs have entirely dominated their lives, retirement in their sixties can be a nightmare; company seminars, courses, professional advice, improving leisure and craft skills, can never fully accomplish what a career executive has known — a reason for living.

It is regrettable that life has to be so single-purposed for so many business and professional people that retirement leaves them floundering, but it is almost the accepted penalty for a work-packed life. Often the response to this penalty is premature death.

Dr Keith Thompson, a Croydon general practitioner with a special interest in the elderly, thinks retirement is just another word for unemployment. 'Men are never ready for it,' he says. 'Women make a social contribution all through their lives, even if they have had careers, whereas men only find prestige through their work. Husbands in retirement often become ciphers. We are much more worried about men than women in retirement.' He notes several

Work After Work

ways in which individuals attempt to handle retirement: 'Some carry on doing the same things, only taking longer over them; others continually decorate the house. Then there is a small professional group — like teachers — who have always been rather terrier-like who go into local housing associations or CND; another group turns itself into great gardeners, and some become culture buffs, travelling the world and writing books about their holidays. Others just sink into the telly.'

Dr Thompson quotes George Bernard Shaw on retirement: 'Shaw said writing was like being an athlete. If you stopped training for a fortnight, you could no longer perform. So, retirement should really be no longer than a fortnight.' So what, then, is the alternative for people with plenty more to give, who have been gently — or not so gently in some cases — evicted from the market place?

Negotiating a later retirement is becoming a ploy of the past, something people used to be able to do to postpone the day of reckoning. Now, with so many jobless, the only honourable route for the over-sixties is towards the exit.

In the ancient world the elders were valued, useful members of the state, and their teaching and advisory functions were prized. They are still prized in the modern world, but beyond the reach of those who really need them because a high financial value is placed on consultants with expertise to offer. Many managers, accountants, lawyers and administrators retire feeling a deep sense of loss — unaware that in the white economy they would be welcomed, needed, appreciated.

Unpaid work was never a viable option for people working in careers, although some exceptional individuals always seem able to squeeze it in alongside full-time jobs. Doing something for nothing has generally been the prerogative of the rich. Who could afford it otherwise?

But, although retirement does not imply freedom from financial worries, for the majority of people it does spell the end of earned income. In planned personal economic terms it also means the end of mortgages and supporting families. With the psychological horizon fixed on managing with a pension which represents less than a previous salary, many people could contemplate the luxury of an

The White Economy and Retirement

expenses-only job in an 'industry' where profit is not the motive. It would be a new and very challenging experience for them. They would first need to be 'debriefed' as they emerge from the commercial world with its emphasis on viability. But they would find many similar organisational problems to tackle. And the bonus is obvious: they would be more in control of how much work they contributed, leaving themselves with the extra free time for relaxing, which traditionally retirement should bestow. Only this way the penalty is not so great. Here is a second case history, which will illustrate this very point:

TONY MOORE

Age 60
Previous occupation A director of Costain International, builders.
Occupation now Adviser to the Bow Baths Community Centre building project, which is converting an old slipper baths into a large social club in Bow, East London.

'I retired a bit early, hastened a little by health problems, and I took advice about what to do with the rest of my life. Someone suggested charity work, but I'd never done anything for nothing! I wrote to REACH and they got me this job overseeing the building work for the Bow project. It is thoroughly interesting and worthwhile, and I think about it a lot. I go to management committee meetings and am in contact regularly with the committee.

'The actual building work is the easiest bit. We had to work out first how much money we would get, then there were legal problems with the lease and negotiating local authority planning regulations, and the Inland Revenue and Charity Commissioners to sort out! I think I've saved them falling into all sorts of traps. I've been careful to see they don't get taken for a ride, and I have a go at hammering contractors to see if I can get a reduction in prices.

Work After Work

'When you are in a career being paid £25,000 with a large staff it is a tremendous responsibility, but this is a personal sort of responsibility, looking after the project's funds, between £70,000 and £80,000, collected by local people. After working a relatively selfish number of years for a major contractor I am enjoying putting something back. When the new centre is completed I shall certainly be applying to REACH again.'

Audrey Shilling, secretary of the management committee, comments:

'Tony has been an enormous help in preparing specifications and supervising builders.

'The slipper baths were built because of the old housing here but it became quickly redundant as new housing with bathrooms was built. The building had been empty five years and had been vandalised. We've not got an architect, but we've learned a lot from Tony. We had a crisis when our original builder pulled out because of cash flow problems and we were back to square one. Tony helped us with new specifications. And he submits certificates of completion of work to the various funding agencies.

'We think it is a good idea to have the help of retired experts. In fact we are going to apply to REACH for a treasurer for the social club when it gets going!'

CHAPTER TWO

THE VOLUNTARY SECTOR

How it began

Today's voluntary world is very different from yesterday's. The first voluntary workers picked up the pieces after the Industrial Revolution had raised Britain's commercial horizons and battered her people. A heavy human price was paid for this outstandingly successful time in our industrial past and it could be argued that the phrase 'social problem' originated then.

The traditional safety net provided by the family and friends' network only really works when people stay in one place. The Industrial Revolution uprooted a mainly agricultural people and flung them to the new factory and mill towns in search of work. There were many social disasters caused by poverty and disease, and the first philanthropic voluntary organisations came into being in response to this suffering. But sympathy and compassion were not automatic in the Victorian era, and the poor were quickly pigeon-holed into those whose misfortune was considered to be of their own making and those who were supposedly 'genuine' victims of circumstance through no weakness of their own. The new voluntary bodies took care of the second category while the punitive Poor Law dealt with the first.

Government stayed mainly out of the picture in these early years, only becoming involved via the back door — when the new industrial society caused death and disease through polluted water and inadequate sewage disposal. Factory and Public Health Acts came first; later came the realisation that the new world needed social help on a national scale. Later, when pensions, unemployment insurance and school meals appeared as part of government

Work After Work

intervention, some of the Victorian ethic still prevailing in the charities was affronted. Blanket benefits for all did not differentiate between those who were worthy of help and those who were not.

A social phenomenon which sprang up towards the end of the nineteenth century was the settlements movement which started in the East End of London. A settlement was an expansive middle class gesture to the poor in which young professional people, usually on their way into the world from university, moved into a building in the very midst of a poor, inner city area, and worked on behalf of the local people.

The purpose of the settlement was to improve the neighbourhood, both educationally and socially. The expertise of the young professionals was freely given to local residents, and as many of them were studying law, the 'poor man's lawyer' service was begun as an early form of citizens' advice bureau. The settlements also acquainted the young middle class with the conditions of poverty. Some, sadly, succumbed to diseases which were rampant in the areas where the settlements were sited.

The mother of all the settlements was Toynbee Hall in Aldgate. Canon Samuel Barnett, the vicar of St. Jude's parish, invited students from Oxford University to join him and his wife in 'living in'. The idea caught on elsewhere and foreign visitors to Toynbee Hall, impressed with this philanthropic experiment, transplanted it to the United States and Europe. They also began to appear in other big English cities such as Manchester and Liverpool.

The settlement movement helped change the law by winning compensation for injured workmen and it promoted clinics for working class people. Some of the settlement workers were inspired by strong religious beliefs, and others were moved by political reform. Both Clement Attlee and William Beveridge, the acknowledged architect of the Welfare State, lived and worked at Toynbee Hall. The students who lived in settlements did not try to 'lower' their standard of living and lived reasonably well, a kind of example to those they were trying to help.

Settlements were the sort of grand concept which would not be viewed favourably in today's climate but they were the genuine forerunners of our neighbourhood centres and participative local groups. Although they were in their heyday in the first twenty years

The Voluntary Sector

of the century they became an umbrella for new charities after statutory social services began. They still exist — Cambridge House settlement in London is famous for its literacy programme — although they are rarely residential now. But Toynbee Hall still has living-in staff; 1984 will be its centenary and interest in this fascinating social development will be revived, especially as an account of its history is being published.

More government help came to ease the poverty of the unemployed after the First World War, and later, during the thirties, unemployment benefits began to be raised through taxation. The voluntary sector took its cue and moved support from easing poverty to making life more bearable for the unemployed. Social clubs were started, and when local authorities built their estates as part of a general housing development, the volunteers were there with tenant associations. Groups specialising in social welfare flourished. The real crossroads was reached with the coming of the Welfare State. The legislation bringing this into being has certainly had its share of criticism. Opponents of what is sometimes contemptuously called the 'nanny state' point to its inability to provide the goods to everybody, while others claim that individual enterprise has been weakened by state provision.

When the Welfare State was born in 1948, the voluntary sector thought its end was nigh. With government now providing social services by statute, was there anything left for the volunteers to do? But twenty years later a report into volunteering by the Aves committee found this arm to be alive and well and reinforcing the Welfare State. Aves discovered that the state itself was in need of volunteers as people's needs increased rather than abated.

During this time the Welfare State seemed to go full circle. In the late forties politicians were saying that the days of charity and voluntary welfare were over. Now voters are being told by politicians that the state not only cannot, but should not, attend to their every need. The message is that independent voluntary activity is necessary to the efficiency and cost effectiveness of the whole state structure, that some jobs are more properly done by willing volunteers than by employees of the state. So the voluntary sector has moved from pioneering the attitudes to care and welfare which prompted the formation of the welfare state, to being viewed as a

Work After Work

necessary — and probably permanent — guarantee of the quality and continued availability of welfare services. There are already a substantial number of activities in which the welfare state has never even sought to replace volunteers with paid employees, so the principle is well established. But will the voluntary sector readily accept such a big extension of its responsibilities, especially in the fields in which it may have called for a more professional service?

The transformation of those volunteers who emerged in the sixties — active and critical of government provision and attempting to inspire improvements — into the unpaid agents of the state may not be entirely smooth. The sixties threw up many critics of government services, like Shelter, the housing pressure group which is still on the scene. Their appearance heralded a change in the voluntary movement; according to Nicholas Hinton, director of the National Council for Voluntary Organisations, 'until then it was becoming a sort of substitute for the State. As a result no new demand has been met by government since the sixties,' he says.

The 1971 Seebohm report on the social services spelled the death of the specialist social worker, to be replaced by one with wider responsibilities. This has left gaps in the care of the young, old and handicapped groups, which voluntary workers have stepped in to cover. 'The state has moved from a direct service provision role to a strategic one, funding and acting as catalyst,' said Hinton. This is where the pioneering spirit of the voluntary world is making its mark. 'The voluntary sector is now providing many more roles, more money and a massive increase in manpower,' he added. It has moved into important areas such as the development of fostering homes, intermediate treatment for youngsters, housing associations and the rehabilitation of alcoholics.

The voluntary sector has a much better relationship with government than either industry or, it would seem, the unions. An increased volunteer force can be interpreted as a move to cut expenditure on some public sector jobs to get social services on the cheap. There were some minor skirmishes involving the use of volunteers during the 1982 health service dispute which betrayed this underlying fear but on the whole these were ironed out.

Most health service unions have an agreed policy with their health districts about the use of volunteer workers. Naturally, the unions

The Voluntary Sector

aim to protect full-time jobs, and most of the full-time jobs in voluntary organisations are filled by paid staff. The TUC says that sensible voluntary groups reach understanding with the relevant unions and take the trouble to see that any scheme they are promoting does not threaten existing workers' paid employment. 'It is my impression,' commented one TUC official, 'that although we are very concerned about jobs being threatened by voluntary labour, most things get smoothed out.'

The view that recruiting more volunteers for social work will stop the state from making statutory provision, and thereby deprive people of work and services, is 'the simple union view' thinks Nicholas Hinton. 'The closer you get to Congress House the more you understand the relationship between us. Most of the voluntary sector full-time paid staff are unionised. And we have to teach our managers industrial relations to handle staff problems involving unions.'

Both Conservative hopes that volunteer labour can save money and Labour fears that it means cut services, are exposed as groundless in a recent study of the future of the Welfare State.[1]

Howard Glennerster, Reader in Social Administration at the London School of Economics, says that the argument that voluntary welfare services will resolve the fiscal restraints on social spending is dubious. 'For local authorities to gain from funding voluntary agencies they would have to be clearly cheaper,' he says. But there is no evidence they are, particularly the larger ones.

And as for the voluntary sector substituting for statutory social services, he insists: 'The more widespread lay involvement and voluntary action there is, the more knowledge there tends to be about the needs of dependent groups and in our experience, the *more* demand for services there is.'

What *is* a charity?

Voluntary groups come in all shapes and sizes. They can be benign and gentle or political and pushy. Some of the newer pressure groups may take radical stands which might set your nerves on edge — or you may find you have a sneaking regard for them. Groups like the National Council for Civil Liberties (NCCL) and the Child Poverty Action Group (CPAG) existed in the fifties but it was not until the sixties that they came into their own and became known as pressure groups, exerting a strong influence on government and public opinion. The distinguishing mark of a pressure group was that it did as much, or more, to change policies as to provide services.

Not all voluntary groups can achieve charitable status, however, particularly the ones which aim to change society. The whole area of charitable status is a minefield for the unwary and the most resilient volunteers can be reduced to confusion by the laws on charity. It is not unusual now for disputes over the use — other than fraudulent — of charitable funds or the credibility of status, to become news. As more groups are tempted into making political judgements about the areas in which they are working, then a common retaliation for those not sharing the views is to question the charitable status of the group.

These assaults occur at both ends of the political spectrum. A research institute, also a registered charity, whose declared aim was the defence of free industrial societies, took offence when an author suggested it was abusing its charitable status by being politically biased (the *Guardian*, 21 August 1981). A university student union — these have charitable status — was recently in trouble with government law officers for using funds on coaches taking members to CND and unemployment demonstrations (*The Times*, 22 January 1983).

Being a charity makes financial sense for a voluntary organisation, but it carries a penalty: the group will not be completely free to say or do what it likes. The modern classification of charity came about during an Income Tax case in 1891. Four aims were designated: the relief of poverty, the advancement of education and of religion, and 'other purposes beneficial to the community'. It is this last category which has caused a lot of the argument over the legal definition of charity. The Charities Act 1960 says charitable purposes means 'exclusively charitable'; in 1980 the Lord Chancellor said the legal concept was not static, but moving and changing.

A charity has the power to employ staff, raise money and own property. It can be run by a small number of people not answerable

The Voluntary Sector

to a membership (trust deed) or it can be an association, which is more appropriate if a membership is needed. The charity trustees will then be the elected committee members who will have management responsibility. A charity may also be incorporated under the Companies Acts as a company limited by guarantee, and a number of organisations appear to favour this. In order to register as a charity, a voluntary group has to convince the Charity Commissioners that its aims are charitable. It is said to be a hard club to join, but once in expulsion is rare. The Commission — three commissioners and six deputies who supervise this sprawling giant — are highly sensitive to objectives of a political nature. Lord Parker spelled it out for them in 1917: 'a trust for the attainment of a political object is not charitable since the Court has no way of judging whether a proposed change in the law will or will not be for the public benefit.'

It is not clear whether political activity is actually tolerated or not, for although politics cannot be the aim of a group applying for registration, political activity ancillary to a non-political aim squeezes in. Hence there is the situation of many charities happily getting on with what seems to be political work — bringing pressure to bear on government to improve conditions for certain sections of society. Similarly, an educational charity can teach about politics but can't be seen to propagate political views. It is that familiar game of knowing how to manipulate the rules without getting into trouble. This situation is summed up by Jeremy Harrison, who has worked for a variety of voluntary organisations in the past ten years:

'Political activity is often interpreted in a pretty subjective way. This came home to me forcibly when in the early seventies I worked within the space of two years for Shelter, campaigning for the homeless and for a whole range of changes in housing policies, even in the laws relating to housing, and then for the National Right to Read Campaign, demanding a whole new attitude — and new money — for teaching adults to read and write.

'At Shelter we campaigned very vigorously and were overtly political. This fuelled a lot of our fund raising by making us very visible. It also greatly enthused our army of volunteers – both the fund raisers and those who were directly trying to help homeless families. We also considered ourselves to be under constant threat of censure, or worse, by the Charity Commissioners and we were warned off a few times. At the Right to Read Campaign we were, if anything, more political. We operated the whole thing from beneath the charitable umbrella of the British Association of Settlements and Social Action Centres. We were not directly trying to raise money. We did not pretend to be trying to make any direct provision for adults who could not read. We used the same publicity techniques that I had used at Shelter.

'We openly demanded changes in policies and the provision of money from government. In the end we got exactly what we wanted. But the big difference was that never once did anyone suggest that we were at risk of abusing or infringing our charitable status.

'I think there are two quite revealing reasons for this: first, we seemed a great deal more respectable than Shelter. You couldn't have put a pin between the relative political opinions of the people involved in the two campaigns, but literacy was somehow a more respectable issue.

'The second reason was that no one ever tried to oppose our views. People found it easy to accept that large numbers of adults could leave school without being able to read and that this was in no way their own fault. No one ever tried to criticise the illiterate for allowing themselves to get into difficulty.

'Most people, however, seemed to be able to find some reason for suggesting that the homeless could have done something to avoid their plight and were therefore less than deserving of help. It was a consistently hard struggle to get over the fact that if there are simply not enough decent homes to go around some people will inevitably be homeless, or will live in rotten slums. It was also hard to convince people that you were not just being clever when you suggested that in such circumstances it was hardly surprising that the people in slums and without homes tended to be those who already had other difficulties and disadvantages.

'I have little doubt that the literacy campaign was allowed to proceed unmolested because it seemed respectable and because no one chose to oppose it. Its methods went unremarked. Shelter's methods were attacked because its message was less comfortable.'

In his study on charity law[2], Francis Gladstone identified the real problem areas as racial harmony, peace and human rights. The

The Voluntary Sector

Charity Commissioners refused to register Amnesty International Trust in 1978, and two years later in the High Court Mr Justice Slade upheld their decision. The Trust had been set up in 1977 to administer the parts of Amnesty's work which could be described as charitable, such as casework.

Sometimes the more outspoken organisations or those dealing with rights have to establish another non-charitable branch separate from their casework in order to publish their views. Conflict over charitable status arises because volunteers often get to a point where they feel on a treadmill — continually helping people who seem to be the victims of a general situation which volunteers are helpless to change.

The Charity Commissioners sometimes rap knuckles themselves if they feel one of their charges is stepping too far out of line regarding political utterances or activities. It also responds to complaints by the public, perhaps those holding opposing views, about a particular charity.

Charities are also sitting targets for sharp investigative journalists seeking out cases of misapplied funds, mismanagement or simple inefficiency. 'Scandals' erupt occasionally as in every other aspect of public life, and they should be out in the open, even if the allegations prove to be groundless. People are — rightly — sensitive about money they give freely and feel particularly cheated if they suspect it is going adrift. The existence of mismanagement scandals over the years has been used as an excuse by the reluctant not to give, so perhaps this is yet more support for the use of retired professionals in the management of the voluntary sector.

The Commissioners registered 3,495 charities in 1981, besides carrying out a lot of work on behalf of existing ones, acting as custodians of property and checking accounts. But what does registration bestow? Money mainly. Grant-making bodies are able to bestow funds. People are encouraged to covenant a donation because you are able to reclaim tax on it; you do not pay Income, Corporation or Capital Gains Tax — if you spend the money on your 'charitable purposes' — and stamp duty on transfers of property to you is halved.

You get rates relief, and providing property you own has been in charitable ownership since September 1974, you are not liable to

Work After Work

Development Land Tax. Although registration is supposed to be compulsory for groups, nothing terrible befalls those who don't except they are denied many benefits. Some foundations are prevented from giving them money because their trust deeds will not allow it. Of course, all the benefits bestowed by registration mean that the Inland Revenue takes a keen interest in who gets registration and whether they are genuinely charitable.

Tony Smythe, a former director of the mental health group MIND, says that charitable status is eagerly sought because of the financial 'goodies'. 'It can be a maze if you don't get it,' he says. 'If a pressure group forms itself into a company in order to raise funds it can get into all sorts of tax difficulties.'

Smythe favours the growth of the smaller community groups now on the scene. 'The big organisations eventually get top-heavy and end up being the sort of body they originally set out to oppose — they end up being like the social services.'

The seventies saw a myriad of pressure groups queueing up for charitable status. Many didn't make it and probably perished as a result. 'Some of the black groups found that they could only do it with white patronage — white lawyers and white sponsors. They got really fed up,' he says.

Applying for registration can be daunting, with not only the legal wizards of the Charity Commission to get past but the thrifty Inland Revenue who naturally do not want to pass up income unchallenged. To take just one example, REACH found an adversary in the Inland Revenue when it applied for registration several years ago. The Revenue's opinion of REACH was that it was 'simply an agency providing a service for bodies which are not necessarily charitable'. Nick Crace, REACH's director, despaired over the letter he received from the Charity Commission passing on the Revenue's feelings. He found himself being compared to the Charitable Catering Society which provided, at cost, catering staff for charities and meals for beneficiaries. REACH was not like groups which were providing educational help to fit out the volunteer for the job:

'The benefit to the executives seemed to be emphasised more than the possible benefits to the organisations making use of them,' considered the Revenue. And it noted that the organisation requesting

The Voluntary Sector

help had to clear some daunting hurdles designed to ensure that the retired executive would not waste time on menial or uninteresting work. This did not constitute true altruism in the eyes of the Revenue: the benefits to the voluntary groups were matched by the benefits to the executives. But the Charity Commission disagreed and took up the case on REACH's behalf, smoothing the way to registration. 'I suspect it was only a token resistance,' said Nick Crace, 'but can you imagine the daunting effect all that would have on little community groups trying for charitable status.'

In his book Francis Gladstone suggests that the voluntary sector needs to provide advocacy and advice for groups applying for registration, and he also supports a form of legal aid fund for groups appealing against refusal of registration.

Some areas of the voluntary sector are taking on the 'charity' issue because they feel the process and the law effectively straitjacket a lot of voluntary effort. But there is some stiff opposition to this from those who fear that 'public' money might subsidise groups spouting their own brand of politics rather than helping to fulfil some public need.

The National Council for Voluntary Organisations (NCVO) has produced a set of proposals for reform. The NCVO points out that while the government is urging charities to help the long term unemployed the Charity Commission is telling them that to do so could endanger their charitable status.

An NCVO working party recommended that the Home Secretary should introduce statutory instruments expanding the aims of charity — race relations, human rights, child welfare in care and unemployment should be included in the charity basket.

As Francis Gladstone suggests, the working party also wants a legal aid fund to allow would-be charities to appeal against unfavourable Commission decisions. But charities should also come out into the open, says the NCVO, and should make accounts available to members of the public.

However, don't get the impression that there is a ferment of change in the voluntary sector. Those organisations already enjoying membership of the 'club' without having to temper their message too much are not overtly enthusiastic about changing the law. As it stands now, the legal definition of a charity, although claimed to be an exclusive definition, is in fact flexible enough for any shrewd organisation to turn to its advantage. And who knows what a new law might do? It is not surprising, therefore, that the Charity Law Reform Committee was 'not exactly welcomed with open arms', says Tony Smythe.

LESLIE WEBB

Age 66

Previous occupation Civil servant working on town and country planning legislation. Mr Webb's last job before retiring was with the Peterborough Development Corporation, where as a principal administrative officer he was involved in the expansion of Peterborough as a new town.

Occupation now Project administrator with the Peterborough Society, which is involved with the preservation of the city's cultural and historical life.

On the surface, it would seem that Mr Webb's professional work, geared to the construction of a modern metropolis, would clash with his voluntary job of preserving the old face of Peterborough. But this is not how it works. 'There's no clash. The Development Corporation and the Society work well together, and the Society's objects fit in very well with my own interests. I've found the job well worth doing, and spend several days a week on it.

'We are trying to persuade the owners of new buildings to put up commemorative plaques with a date — we are even asking home-owners to do this. We want to find someone to make the stones and we hope to sell them to help the Society.'

Wilfred Court, retiring secretary of the Society added: 'We like to be independent from the City Council and the Development Corporation so that we are not inhibited in what we say. But we work well with both of them. Peterborough was already a large city before the twenty-year development plan; the

The Voluntary Sector

infrastructure and social organisation were already there, unlike some of the other new towns such as Harlow or Stevenage.

'The Society makes representations on a number of proposals about new buildings. Leslie Webb and I had already worked together in the past, on a city centre improvement committee — me representing the city's architects and he seconded from the Development Corporation. Now he is fitting in well to the Society's work and has proved valuable to us.'

Not a one-way deal

The world of voluntary action is in its way as fraught and entrepreneurial as the commercial and professional worlds. Groups can spring into life one day and crash the next, just like a business. Many of them that did so would have survived to help some section of society if they only had more business know-how.

Some of the large organisations stay alive in much the same way as big fish in the public sector — their 'bankruptcy' would be unthinkable — but their survival continues in an atmosphere of muddle and hit-and-miss management. Yet how can the voluntary sector be exposed more to current management theory and practice *and* retain its uniquely supportive and profit-free role? This problem has taxed many fine brains in industry, government and the voluntary sector. It is acknowledged that efficient management is a must for the future, but the very idea of the white economy rubbing shoulders with commerce makes volunteers uneasy. But, rather than recommending a simple grafting of the latest management concepts on to the sector, it could be argued that business and commerce could use something the volunteers have in abundance: 'If only British industry had some of the elements of the management of survival that these groups have!' insists Nicholas Hinton. Yet there is resistance amongst volunteers to having commercial management solutions imposed upon their problems. A 1978 Gallup survey on management in the voluntary sector showed that its workers saw themselves as distinctly different from commercial organisations.

Work After Work

Most were satisfied with their management structure, only 12 per cent were interested in in-service training, and even less wanted management consultancy.

But the National Council of Voluntary Organisations (NCVO) was mindful of the organisational difficulties of the sector and set up a working party to review the situation, under the chairmanship of a business academic, Professor Charles Handy. The working party took a look at the Gallup survey and discovered it was mainly concerned with the views of directors. But a trip down the management hierarchy produced a different picture:

'No-one willingly admits to mismanagement in his own organisation,' the report said. But the working party found that using the word 'management' hampered them in their investigation as it conjured up a different world of values which couldn't be applied to the voluntary sector. The investigators switched to 'effectiveness'.[4]

Handy found that merely muddling through was not good enough and in fact was increasingly seen as inadequate. The organisations ran into many difficulties. For example, management functions were often carried out by board members who, by the nature of the game, were part-timers. There were, too, often dilemmas surrounding the leadership — should it be personal or participative in a modern fashion? What about changing direction as new problems arose which conflicted with old ideals? There were different aims within single groups: management committees looked outside to sponsors, staff looked inward to clients. Were there any ways of checking if groups met their targets? The Gallup survey had recorded that three-quarters of the respondents agreed that appraisal was important, but only one-quarter claimed to be doing it already.

Businesses have their profits as a guide to performance but there is no such test in volunteering, and Handy found a reluctance to play the numbers game. One project director, asked how effective was the work done by his volunteers with alcoholics, replied sharply, 'if this project saves one alcoholic then it has been successful'.

Everyone, from the client up to the management committee, should know where their group is going, the report declared. Otherwise underlying disagreements about its purpose would spring up into trivial friction which would distract volunteers and absorb time and energy.

The Voluntary Sector

At the end of the report Handy admitted that some new thinking was needed to find appropriate ways of organising voluntary groups and the party's recommendations reflected this realisation. But they did not suggest a single solution to the sector's management problems, such as one body to advise the whole 'industry', but a brokerage function for the NCVO. A regional network of key people in voluntary work would offer information on relevant management courses either designed specially for groups or planned by colleges and polytechnics with the groups in mind.

Handy also suggested that more consultancy be made available to volunteers.

The report's recommendations have been taken seriously by NCVO which has set up a management development unit in London responsible for starting the regional networks. It has a staff of three whose salaries are paid for by the Council and the main funding is from the Department of Health and Social Security (DHSS), the Home Office Voluntary Services Unit, and several trusts. Jenny Hill, who works for the unit, takes a bullish view of the extent to which industry could learn from the voluntary sector:

'We could teach them! Industry regards the sector as 'woolly' but we can manage on slim resources. This is not a one-way deal, with business providing answers for the amateurs.'

Nonetheless, organisational skills are badly needed:

'These groups are difficult to run. They are under-resourced and the fact that the people in them want to see something done does not mean they are good at doing it.

'The managers have to rely on volunteers with little experience. How would a manager from industry like to handle staff who are unpaid so you've no control over them? There are none of the carrots and sticks of industry.

'The group must also know how to manage relationships with constituents, funders and other voluntary groups – and they have to get their product right.'

There are, nonetheless, problems that industry and the voluntary sector share, like being a good employer. Paid and unpaid staff mingle in voluntary groups, sometimes creating tensions. The paid staff, often with a social work background, belong to unions and want reasonable conditions of work. They may bristle at having to

Work After Work

work late at meetings which are organised to accommodate lay committee members. They may also demand better expense allowances from their committees — and find themselves rebuffed. There is often more understanding between ex-industry volunteers and paid workers. On the other hand, unpaid workers do not like the idea of management, wanting to work creatively and co-operatively.

Jenny Hill thinks that anyone expecting volunteers to provide cheap social services has got it all wrong. 'This will never be a cheap option,' she says, 'it needs underpinning with money if it is going to be effective. During the seventies when there was more money around a lot of paid workers were taken on and they are still there.'

So what help can business 'professionals' give? For a start, the voluntary world needs help with modern technology — with devising better information systems on a sound basis, so that money will not be spent on something rapidly obsolete; it needs better ways of interviewing and selecting clients and staff; it is desperately short of marketing skills now that charities are moving into the retail trade; public relations skills are paramount to most groups, which are in the business of communication. Very few of them get this right.

In technical management the needs are overwhelming. Vehicle and building maintenance are just two needs: think of play-buses, coaches for the elderly, hospital visiting vehicles, buildings that need repair and upkeep.

Most groups need help with budgeting. Fund raising is a specialist job which some in industry might adapt to — and some might not. Accountancy skills are easier to provide. Voluntary groups need the sort of accountant who can think about goals and translate them into financial terms, rather than be too absorbed about immediate difficulties.

These are problems needing practical, on-the-spot help. The wider management issues also need specialist assistance, but the volunteers are trying to tackle this themselves. NCVO runs management courses with Industrial Society lecturers covering a wide range of subjects from fund-raising tactics and employment law to handling committee meetings. Other organisations are getting wise to the need to train lay managers and are also running courses.

The whole scope of volunteering is broadening, with the simple 'helping people' motive cutting little ice, especially with some

The Voluntary Sector

of the new community schemes. Commendable motives with no organisational back-up can be more of a hindrance to the people requiring the service. 'Can you imagine,' asks Jenny Hill, 'one of the Community Projects being organised in a little village somewhere? It can be quite something for them to get it to the required standard.'

But with the right match of volunteer with appropriate skills and project needing them, a stimulating experience can ensue. Jenny Hill is an enthusiast: 'Business people could find it fascinating working in this world; it could be much more interesting than anything they've done in their whole careers. It would be impossible for them to see it merely as another job.'

GEORGE ROSE

Age 66
Previous occupation Factory accounting manager.
Present occupation Handling finance for the Coventry Cyrenians, a voluntary group of young people trying to put roofs over the heads of the single homeless, or vagrants, as they are more often called.

'All I knew about the Cyrenians before I took this job was that I didn't like the "single homeless" because they always shouted at me whenever I passed one of their hostels in Coventry. Now I've been doing the job I realise there's no-one else looking after them and the Cyrenians are very necessary.

'The Cyrenians try to rehabilitate people if possible. They have about five houses and a hostel for providing shelter while people are on the move. I look after the social security and local authority money which is allocated to the single homeless for overnight lodging. There is quite a bit of administration handling these cheques and the Cyrenians have some full-time people. I go to monthly management committee meetings and account the final balance sheet.

'The Cyrenians are pretty astute, they know what's due to

Work After Work

them. It's surprising what people miss out on just because they don't know what money they are entitled to. My mother had a shop so I've been brought up on figures.

'I work about half a day a week for them, and I'm also a treasurer for a community centre. My old firm recently decided to start a social club for its former employees and they have had an enormous response. It's amazing how lonely people get when they retire. Some people don't talk to anyone for weeks except the rent collector.

'I still get shouted at by the single homeless in Coventry but I feel differently about them now.'

The Cyrenian's chairman, solicitor Robert Zara, comments: 'It's an excellent idea putting retired professional people in touch with people who need them. We're happy with him and hope he's happy with us.'

---

[1]*The Future of the Welfare State: Remaking Social Policy.* Edited by Howard Glennerster. Heinemann Educational Books.
[2]*Charity, Law and Social Justice*, Francis Gladstone, Bedford Square Press. £4.95.
[3]*Charity Law, a case for change?* NCVO Charity Law Working Group. Free from NCVO Legal Department, 26 Bedford Square, London WC1.
[4]*Report of the Charles Handy Working Party on Improving Effectiveness in Voluntary Organizations.* National Council for Voluntary Organisations, 75p

CHAPTER THREE

INDUSTRY: COMING IN OUT OF THE COLD

Youth unemployment has finally driven British industry out of the closet and into the community. Our American counterparts are well ahead in giving help and money to social enterprises — perhaps because statutory provision is less there — but apart from the big Quaker companies there is no particular tradition in this country of firms involving themselves in local matters outside the factory gate. This is now changing.

Government and the voluntary sector have mounted an onslaught on industry to accept a social role in training young people. In 1983 full-page national newspaper advertisements appeared, tugging at companies' consciences to help in the training programme. The adverts were couched in fairly strong terms, accusing companies of being hypocritical if they paid lip service only to the concept of better trained youth with brighter job prospects, and warning of the demise of British industry without a proper training programme.

'Community' is a vague term, loosely referring to the area outside hospital and prison. It has become an umbrella description implying a co-ordinated social geography, but many people who are supposedly living under this 'umbrella' are sceptical of its existence.

Peter Stubbings, deputy director of the Volunteer Centre has asked if the 'community' is beginning to feel conned. 'The answer to this question must be, in part, yes,' he says. 'And those of us encouraging neighbourhood care are collaborators in it. We express the confidence trick in various ways. We talk about supporting informal systems, about empowering the community, about interweaving, about the continuum of care, about helping ordinary people to help each other.'

The language is warm and comfortable, complains Mr Stubbings,

Work After Work

'yet we don't know much about whether these things actually work.' The community certainly will float unless anchored by a commitment from those living and working it it. Until an initial agreement is reached between these two groups about its existence, it can hardly be more than mere streets and buildings. One of the most important steps in this agreement must come from industry, especially in areas where firms are reducing their workforces and leaving a trail of unemployment.

May we borrow your accountant?

The movement to remind industry of its responsibility really started ten years ago with the setting up of an organisation called Action Resource Centre (ARC). This industry-backed group began with the idea of seconding personnel from the private sector to help local schemes get off the ground. There was some tradition of secondment in industry — local councillors and magistrates were often allowed time from work at managers' discretion — but ARC got the ball rolling on personnel 'loans' and in the past five years this idea has flourished. But it is going further. ARC realised that secondment was just one of the options to lure industry into the outside world: 'We've loosened our stays,' admits ARC's director Cecilia Allen. 'We are now trying to find ways that companies can help their local communities other than by full secondment, which sometimes puts them off. We want to persuade commitment to certain projects and sometimes the best way to work is to go along to a company and say 'you have three accountants — may we borrow one for an afternoon?'

When a company makes hundreds of workers redundant ARC asks: 'What are you giving back?' And more companies are getting the point. 'The tradition of employment in some places is a thing of the past,' says Ms Allen. 'We are into creating more work where we can although it won't always provide jobs as such.'

ARC operates regionally, with full-time managers, and is approached by voluntary and community projects who need help with their schemes. The agency works to guidelines — schemes wanting its help must be reflecting local needs, not be offering unfair

Industry: Coming in Out of the Cold

competition, must recognise training as preparation not work-substitution, avoid duplication of other schemes, recognise the need for good management and be properly researched. In other words, ARC is nobody's fool.

It puts its weight behind good, useful schemes which have a chance of success. When the agency has decided to help it circulates the scores of big companies who support it. ARC regularly keeps its work in their eyes by a shrewd public relations effort, but specific projects needing help are given stronger promotion. 'A job specification for the necessary secondee is written up — and then we start a trawl,' says Ms Allen. 'Sometimes we have to wait, sometimes we chivvy.'

ARC takes management personnel from several stages of career development: those in mid-career, probably in their forties who have been doing their job some time and no doubt in need of refreshment; high flyers between 25 and 35 who will see the ARC challenge as a proving ground for their developing abilities — 'these are great for us,' says Ms. Allen; and those executives in their early fifties whose job runs out but have several years to go before their companies' pension policy comes into force.

Cecilia Allen acknowledges that job creation is getting tougher. The agency is now moving into the complex business of creating work where possible for the disabled and handicapped, getting money from local authorities and the Manpower Services Commission. In Birmingham ARC has taken advantage of the fact that a company repairing hearing aids for the DHSS was overstretched. With the help of the city council and MSC a workshop has been established for a team of disabled workers to repair hearing aids. 'We hope it will become a viable company,' says Ms Allen; 'there is no reason why it shouldn't go like a bomb.'

Seconded resources were used in this venture, in surveys carried out on its potential, but they were not 'clear cut secondees' on a fixed term. And companies gave premises and equipment.

In Leicester a report is being prepared on job opportunities for disabled workers. Discussions are going on with local firms about their policy regarding employment for the handicapped. 'This may well end up in an organisation seeking work for the disabled, and we'll need a secondee to head it up,' says Ms Allen.

Work After Work

Secondment undoubtedly shakes up people coming from commerce and industry and their reactions are mixed. One man from the Pru wrote in an ARC newsletter that he was thoroughly enjoying himself as a personnel adviser to the National Association of Community Relations Councils but 'I came expecting to utilise my specialist personnel skills and have already realised how shallow those skills are when put into a generalist environment.'

Another young Prudential employee gave part-time accountancy help to the Lambeth Mobile Creche Project, sponsored by the Lady Margaret Hall Settlement. The 1981 riots, plus the Scarman report, pointed up the need for help in Brixton and this persuaded her that anything she could do to help the borough would be worthwhile. She says, 'Right from the start of my secondment I thought in terms of "we", not the project and me.'

ARC feels that companies tend to play down their community involvement and many employees are in ignorance of what their firms are up to in the outside world. 'Let your personnel know,' urges Ms Allen. The first employees might hear of a company secondment scheme is when asked to join it. They can sometimes be alarmed at the prospect.

Industry may be picking up the invitation to give some of its skills and resources just when the same economic afflictions hitting the community are blighting it also. A generous secondment policy may already be regarded by some corporations as a luxury: an investment of up to £40,000 with nil return — on the balance sheet that is.

Future prospects for secondment

'Secondment is drying up,' thinks Nicholas Hinton of NCVO, 'but companies are being drawn ever more into socially responsible programmes. In the future a successful company will be judged not just on its financial success but on its social audit, on what it does for a community. There are indications of pressures on companies to behave in this way, and a company not involved in some sort of training will be considered out of gear.'

Not everyone agrees that the recession will kill off longer term secondment. Stephen O'Brien, who heads Business in the Com-

Industry: Coming in Out of the Cold

munity, is convinced that the demand for good secondees is outstripping supply. 'I may be a lone voice in this,' he admits. 'Ten years ago there were a couple of firms in the field — IBM and Marks and Spencer were the first. Then others noticed and followed. At first people used it for placing people who were just short of retirement — they were using secondment to solve *their* problems and the people were not always adequate.

'Things are more developed now and it is possible to sell the idea to companies. The sales pitch is — it's good for business. Being in the community broadens staff, is better than keeping them in their narrow patch, and develops their careers.'

Mr O'Brien is a former chairman of an international money broking firm. He has a long involvement with the voluntary sector and sees it undergoing a dramatic change. 'The private donor is fading away and most groups are getting statutory money, which is forcing them to work more professionally.'

Business in the Community often co-operates with ARC on local projects. It exists as local enterprise agencies which advertise their services in local papers and offers help to small businesses starting up or running into trouble. It also helps the self-employed and becomes involved with youth training. Underlying the philosophy of this organisation, which is sponsored by private and public money, is a sense of responsibility for the unemployed.

The British Steel Corporation set up BSC (Industry) Ltd to attract new industries to areas where it has shut down factories or made redundancies. During the past three years BSC Industry has given money to 600 businesses and 16,500 new jobs have been created.

Says Stephen O'Brien: 'The riots we had in Britain showed us all what happens if an effort is not made. We all thought it could happen in Los Angeles but not here. This message has been realised by companies.'

Marks and Spencer finds that its short-term secondment policy helps employees to flex their skills in a different setting and the experience gives them a lasting interest in social problems. The company generally helps projects in the areas where its staff work and live. It is mainly concerned with job creation via help to small businesses, and youth training, but senior and junior staff are

Work After Work

loaned to local projects such as Brixton United, which is a task force to ensure community ideas get started. One of their export managers recently spent 18 months managing a training workshop in Southwark, run by the Burnbake Trust, which tries to give young offenders a commercial goal. Many Marks and Spencer staff have been borrowed for Project Fullemploy which teaches clerical skills to young people who otherwise would be badly prepared to face the job market.

Secondment in action

Jeff Armstrong was seconded from his company Elida Gibbs, where he was general sales manager, to set up a project under the new Youth Training Scheme. He has had 34 years of selling and is in the last few years of his career with the company. His scheme will take 100 16-year-olds through a year of learning about life and social skills — ordinary things like setting up bank accounts — and give them experience in selling. Quite simply, he was chosen because: 'When the CBI appealed to industry to help with this scheme my company decided that it was best at the business of selling and I was assigned to set up a scheme in Islington.' Mr Armstrong's students will be taught some basic merchandising techniques, including the operation of electronic tills. 'This is essential,' he says. 'I've recruited hundreds of salesmen in my time and none of them had any basic selling experience.'

Islington was chosen because, like many other London boroughs, 'it was sitting on a powder keg. I didn't want to set it up in Brixton because you trip over all the welfare workers there. But this scheme can be applied universally.'

The students will spend 23 weeks at a further education college and 26 weeks 'on the job' — working in stores and merchandising agencies. Mr Armstrong had to recruit tutors for the budding young sales force, secretarial staff for the scheme, and find premises with furniture. 'The fact that a youngster can't leave school and go and get a job is one of the biggest social problems we've got,' he says. 'I feel I am involved in missionary work. People talk about "bloody kids" but do they know their problems? There is a lot of prejudice about.' Jeff Armstrong's scheme will need funding to the tune of £240,000, a sum which includes paying the students £25 a week, plus some fares. He says: 'You have to find a roof over their heads, somewhere for them to sit down, towels, soap, all that sort of thing. Other companies might contribute.'

Secondment's impact on society

What is happening in the 'social audit' of business is not nearly enough to make a significant impression on the majority of jobless, but a precedent has been set, and fashions grow. Sir Alastair Pilkington says that no sector can sensibly contract out of concern for economic and social problems. 'It is in our own interests and that of our firms to support projects that improve the well-being of the community,' he says.

And concern for the young in our jobless society will inevitably spread to the workers at the other end of the spectrum who are being dislodged from work prematurely.

Companies will find themselves pressurised to accept some responsibility towards people being pushed out of jobs in their forties to make way for the young as the labour market carries on shrinking. Pre-retirement courses are an attempt to help the middle-aged-plus, but they are woefully underpowered and often misconceived.

The Manpower Services Commission has set itself and others the huge task of providing a new system of training and education for working life for every sixteen-year-old school leaver — at least for every one who cannot move straight into a job, which means the overwhelming majority of them. The long-term effect of this on the workings of the labour market and on the activities of industry, which is expected to sponsor the vast majority of this training, was only guessed at when the Youth Training Scheme was launched. It is expected that more than 400,000 places will be available, and this represents a massive change affecting the expectations of both employers and young people.

Work After Work

Putting secondment in perspective

Nothing works perfectly. Retired executives getting a second wind and refreshing mid-career secondment sounds like the answers to a number of prayers. But there are obstacles to these potentially fine ideas which have to be faced if they are not to be written off as impractical. Principally, there is the problem of the yawning divide between the two worlds which this book is suggesting be bridged. The workers who people these worlds may be total strangers to each other, with different views, methods of working and expectations. On the face of it, clashes of temperament seem inevitable.

There is a notion that an individual with very high skills will automatically benefit the voluntary sector. But the sector resists this, insisting that without careful matchmaking the experience can be fluffed. High flying secondees can crash-land psychologically because of the stark contrast between their tightly scheduled and mutually supportive commercial life and the unstructured atmosphere of a community project where they must be self-motivated from morning to night. The more cosseted an executive from industry is, the more shattering the transition. Promising executives have fallen at this first hurdle.

Voluntary personnel are aware of the danger. Cecilia Allen of ARC feels some pre-secondment training is needed — perhaps one day a week spent in the chosen project before joining it fully. There has also been the suspicion that companies unload people into secondment who they would rather not have in the business, for a variety of reasons. Everyone bristles with indignation at this prospect, notably Cecilia Allen: 'As far back as 1973 when we started we saw this danger of being a dumping ground,' she says. 'We just said simply "no deadwood or we'll send them back!" Strangely enough, some of the more difficult people we've helped place, who must have been the bane of their colleagues' lives and murder to work with, have slotted beautifully into community schemes.'

Marks and Spencer has written into its code of practice that secondment must not be a dumping ground for people not required, or being appraised. As they point out, it would not only reflect badly on the company but there would still be a problem when the secondment came to an end.

Industry: Coming in Out of the Cold

A major worry for the voluntary organisation is what to do with a talented executive. A prize catch can leave the group perplexed as to the exact nature of work to be carried out: job specification has yet to arrive in the voluntary sector. To cope with this, agencies like REACH and ARC insist on accurate job descriptions to offer applicants. They deal with the executives and they know this is what is needed. Badly drawn up specifications do not attract good 'staff'. But this is also the nub of the problem, because 'job specification' is business language and not generally spoken in the other sector.

A way round this is for go-betweens like REACH to translate the charities' needs into the required format, although some fairly expert interviewing is needed to figure out exactly what they want.

'In an ideal world we should be able to help them,' says Nick Crace at REACH, 'but we are too small at present and can't allow this level of involvement. It is a bit of a harsh doctrine but we just can't go in for this sort of help at the moment. I sometimes see an incompetent, badly worded job description and I choke down my impatience because these are exactly the people who need executive skills more than anyone else.

'We do sometimes spoonfeed people on the telephone and we encourage the volunteers to go and do a bit of digging themselves — go along and ask some questions, even if at the outset the job doesn't look very promising.

'Obviously our ambition *is* to help the charities in this way, to be a sort of ACAS between the two groups. But ACAS is a longwinded operation needing tremendous amounts of manpower, and we can't be in this league yet.'

But the REACH matchmakers have learned some of the short cuts to happy job-placing. Joan Simmons, one of the three agency matchers, feels that if charities play their cards right they can land themselves good staff. 'A wise charity coaxes good people in and then uses their skills,' she says. Unwise organisations ask for senior people, 'then won't let them do anything'.

Some of the confusion about work roles can end up with a group demanding a chartered accountant when a bookkeeper is what they really need; 'groups with a small turnover don't need chartered accountants. And often qualified accountants aren't in this market because they can always do a little work after their retirement.'

Work After Work

Job titles are as important as they are in the salaried sector: nobody wants to be a 'treasurer' with its implications of working at home alone. 'People want to be "financial advisers",' says Ms Simmons. Sometimes she is in the difficult position of having to tout a specialist around the charities, perhaps with knowledge of complex matters like Capital Transfer Tax and Stamp Duty, because no-one is sure how to use them properly.

'One charity wanted help with marketing,' she recalls, 'but when the person with marketing skills arrived they found they had to sort out administration. The next thing was the charity ringing up and asking for marketing help again. "Are we allowed two?" they asked.'

The more enthusiastic REACH applicants may go along to a charity and find a chaotic scene. 'They may think — "this is something I can get my teeth into. I can really do something here — anything I do can only bring an improvement!".'

Problems also arise when an executive may not actually want to use the skills that have comprised a career. Bank managers are notorious for not wanting to do anything with figures. Here again, diplomacy must enter into the picture, and professional skills may start to be used once the applicant has seen how much a particular charity needs them.

'In a developing charity it is difficult to be precise,' explains Major-General Robert Loudoun, director of the Mental Health Foundation. 'REACH wants a detailed job description before it produces anyone and I've tried but it is so difficult to be exact. There are so many jobs to be done, we want people who will suggest new ways of doing things. It will depend a lot on the strengths of the person who joins us. We want someone with a clear head for administration who can talk to people, some personality to carry it off.'

'Fund-raiser' is another job description REACH particularly steers clear of. It conjures up tin-rattling tactics and it's not a job anyone wants. Charities badly want funds but the actual job of packaging their image in order to draw donations is much more complex than fund-raising implies. 'People say "we need a money-raiser", but that's a downmarket job,' says Helen Reeves, national officer of the National Association of Victim Support Schemes. 'What it really means is that the organisation needs to be sold to

Industry: Coming in Out of the Cold

business — put across in language that will translate good social work practice into good business sense. We need help with the image; it's not as straightforward as being a fund-raiser.'

Ms Reeves says groups get disgruntled when they need cash and tend to ask bluntly for someone to raise it. This conjures up a post involving the writing of endless letters to people requesting handouts. 'What we really need is someone to teach us how to sell ourselves. How to organise the way we look to commercial firms. Do we look trustworthy? They may see us as a selection of vicars and social workers and they may ask — "who will look after the money?" Will we invest it? Will we fritter it away and what are our long-term plans? Trusts and commercial bodies may ask us these questions and we have no answers.' Written up like this the job may come over more attractively to a recruit from business.

Fund raising can have its subtle side. Mr Dave Rai, a sixty-two-year-old retired diplomatic administrator, gave some voluntary help to the social services unit of the famous church of St Martin-in-the-Fields, London which involved some clever manoeuvring. The unit has been in business helping those down on their luck since the early part of the century. It runs a day centre for the unemployed and homeless, a bed-sitter hostel, a soup kitchen — and a unique emergency scheme whereby local authorities can apply to the unit for funds to help individual 'clients' who fall between their own rules. The Church provides £70,000 a year for this relief fund, and so needs to raise money itself to keep it going. Mr Rai was drafted in to help the unit director Norman Ingram-Smith attempt to persuade those local authorities who had been on the receiving end of the fund, to dip into their budgets to keep this excellent scheme going:

'We send local authorities in London who apply on behalf of individuals and families, thousands of pounds for ancient dossers and alcoholics — those people social workers can't help financially,' says Mr Ingram-Smith. 'So we sent out letters requesting help from thirty of the boroughs who have used the fund. Mr Rai and I drafted the request. This sort of grant-getting is a technical activity. It's not begging — something I wouldn't be able to do — it's more like stalking the corridors of power.'

Both General Loudoun and Ms Reeves agree that there is a different way of doing things in the voluntary world. 'The bosses

Work After Work

may be from the social work world, or be vicars or medics,' she says. 'They won't be 9 to 5. They'll be prepared to work evenings and weekends — but they'll come in at lunchtime, not very businesslike.

'They don't write things down and they don't write up the business diary. They'll put their expenses in a month late. They may be thinking this way as a value judgement! They may say proudly — "I may not be a good administrator but I know how to talk to people!" — but someone from business will know how important administration is and there would be a clash of values.'

She feels that education is needed in the voluntary sector to use the skills of retired business employees 'and to respect those skills'.

The independent Victim Support Schemes around the country are run mainly by volunteers, many of them retired teachers, police and probation officers and social workers, 'They know the field already and come along to sit on management committees or to take part in visiting victims,' she says. Referrals to local schemes are made by police, and volunteers visit victims of assault and burglary to offer advice — or just to talk.

'We wouldn't survive without our volunteers,' says Ms Reeves, who is enthusiastic about retired business people taking regular jobs in groups like hers. 'From the manpower and job satisfaction point of view it's fantastic. For intelligent, active people of sixty or more, not to be able to use their skills is appalling when there is so much work to be done, especially in the caring field. We need them badly, but we'll have to do something about the communication problem. Business language is so different from ordinary, everyday working language.'

The National Association has the services of Mr Ronald Chick, retired managing director of an oil company who came to them from REACH and tackles insurance, tax and other administration work. Ms Reeves is full of praise for her admin officer: 'He's marvellous,' she says.

General Loudoun, who had not as yet employed a retired executive, said that he foresaw problems arising when the man or woman from commerce or industry, who had been well served clerically and secretarially, arrived in a much less organised office.

'Here we do everything ourselves,' he pointed out. 'We write our

Industry: Coming in Out of the Cold

own letters, make our own coffee, do our own filing. Charities have little money, especially when they are starting up, for the luxury of administrative support. We operate on a shoestring. What you are doing is begging and you have to get over any diffidence about that. You must also be wholeheartedly behind the aims of the charity you go to work for. That's the job satisfaction, seeing its aims being forwarded.'

When REACH conducted a survey of its placements in 1981 some of the comments made by retired executives who had gone into voluntary jobs centred around the basic divergence of work expectation. Some of the REACH-placed workers spoke of feeling 'under-utilised', of not being useful enough, of not having enough work to do. Behind their remarks lay a lifetime of functioning in an ordered business atmosphere where work was organised and where they knew what their jobs were. They expected to continue to function this way and to a certain extent REACH believes they are right to expect it.

These are some of the snags that arise when business and community try to co-operate. But that is all they are — snags — and not beyond the competence of both sides to smooth out. The concept of more social involvement of companies is being pushed forward all the time and white collar workers will become increasingly familiar with outside schemes and voluntary workers. Nicholas Hinton's advice to anyone with a few years to go before retirement is to have a look at what your company is doing now, and perhaps have a few trial runs to prepare for a second career later on.

BILL EVANS

Age 70
Previous occupation Factory owner, producing steel parts for refrigerators.
Occupation now Teaching sixteen-year-old boys the skills of tool making at the Intaskill training centre in Warley, near Birmingham, which is a Community Projects Foundation scheme supported by the Manpower Services Commission.

Work After Work

'I had my own factory for eighteen years in Scotland but it went bust,' says Bill Evans, 'so at the retiring age of sixty-five I came back to my roots in the West Midlands. I couldn't just sit at home. I had a couple of inventions in my mind and I looked around for some means of making the tools to manufacture the patented products. I was told about Intaskill, but I thought they'd say "no go". Instead, they welcomed me. Now I'm teaching lads how to make tools. Toolmaking is a highly skilled job and you have to sort out the promising ones who want to learn. You have to be a certain temperament to be a good toolmaker, unexcitable and patient. Some of the lads go on to get jobs after they've learned.

'The boys are making the tools to produce one of my inventions, a remedial wall tie for buildings which is designed to replace rusted ones. I also have another prototype — a dart sharpener — which has aroused a lot of interest.

'I come to the centre every day as I have done for three years. I wouldn't be doing anything else. I think there are a lot of people like me with a vast amount of knowledge which could be wasted. I don't get paid but I do have claim on the tools, and I will receive royalties from the products when they are manufactured.'

Intaskill's former project director Arthur Heel comments:

'The youngsters get two sides of the coin from Bill — he can develop shopfloor skills as well as those which he has as a result of being director of his own firm. I would like to see more of this type of involvement in training by retired business people. Young people are much more inclined to take advice from someone in the 65 plus group than they are from the middle-aged.

'Young and old get on well together — it's the young and middle-aged who don't hit it off.

'There is terrific interest in Bill's dart sharpener from some of the top darts players and our dream — which looks like becoming a reality — is that some of our youngsters will get jobs in its manufacture. And we hope the same thing will happen with the wall tie too.'

Useful addresses
Volunteer Centre 29 Lower King's Road, Berkhamsted, Herts. Tel. 04427-73311.
Action Resource Centre Henrietta House, 9 Henrietta Place, London W1. Tel. 01-629 3826/7
Business in the Community 227a City Road, London EC1V 1JU. Tel. 01-253 3716
Project Fullemploy Robert Hyde House, 48, Bryanston Square, W.1. Tel. 01-262-2405/6/7.
Mental Health Foundation 8/10 Hallam Street, London W.1. Tel. 01-580-0145.
National Association of Victim Support Schemes 34 Electric Lane, Brixton, London SW9. Tel. 01-737 2010.
Social Services Unit St Martin-in-the Fields Church. Tel. 01-930 4137/1781.

CHAPTER FOUR

GETTING THE JOB

Retirement is looming. Your new leisure agenda is welcoming, but already you are aware it won't absorb your entire timetable. You are attracted to the idea of seeing how the voluntary sector operates and perhaps joining in. How do you go about it?

You can go along to the offices of the charity in your high street, or the local charity shop, or contact a branch of a voluntary organisation which you are familiar with. But this can be a disastrous introduction to the voluntary sector because more likely than not you risk a snub. Most groups are not geared to the walk-in volunteer in much the same way manufacturers are not organised to deal directly with customers. Much of the job of matching the bulk of the willing with the wanting is effectively done by local Volunteer Bureaux and local Councils for Voluntary Service (see page 64) but there has always been a difficulty about matching scarce, sometimes specialist, abilities with specific needs. It is in appreciation of the frustration caused by a failure to do this that REACH now offers a service exclusively to retired executives. For them it is a short route to finding the people most in need of their professional skills and experience.

REACH opened shop in 1979 when Nicholas Crace, a former deputy director of MIND, talked the idea over with friends from industry. They knew the idea was a good one because no government or commercial agency was covering this field. Executives retired and either followed a pattern of more leisure or tried, sometimes unsuccessfully, to fix themselves up with paid or unpaid part-time work. There were no go-betweens to rescue many from the 'empty diary' syndrome.

REACH started during a period when the retirement age was

Getting the Job

being brought forward, both compulsorily and voluntarily, at an increasingly fast rate. People have begun to finish their paid careers at a time of their life when they would be most valuable. At a seminar which the agency held in 1982, John Sykes, group personnel adviser of Booker McConnell Ltd, talked of the 'casualties of circumstance' — those persons made redundant after long service. 'They may be virtually unemployable today,' he said, 'not through any fault of their own.' It was possible that over a million of the 10 million retired people in Britain were managerial or professional. Many had retired early, in good health. At his own company, between 1975–79, over a quarter of retiring employees did so early.

To these professionals, REACH could be a lifeline. The agency is growing quickly. Its 1983 budget of £70,000 was contributed by business, charitable trusts and the Home Office Voluntary Services Unit.

Since it began, REACH has handled 2,300 applications for work, and 2,500 requests for personnel from the voluntary sector. At the close of 1983, 700 volunteers had been matched, 800 had withdrawn, 300 were in the process of negotiation and 500 were available.

Nearly everyone who applies to REACH is offered something within three weeks. In its own survey of placements made during the latter part of 1981, the agency found that forty matches — half the total of matches in that period — were considered to be successful by at least one partner. Particularly happy, says REACH's researcher Frances Bone, were the organisations.

Ms Bone's survey showed that most respondents were pleased with the free service offered — a third of both volunteers and organisations rating it 'very good'.

A prospective volunteer who contacts REACH is sent a detailed form to fill out and some information about the agency. If the form comes back filled up — the volunteer is serious — it is fed into a computer and the volunteer is scored with attributes which helps to match job and applicant. The computer suggests job possibilities in print-outs for each applicant. Wide selections emerge with some humorous side-effects — like the lifelong brewer who prompted a suggestion of a job with the Band of Hope from the computer! A REACH matchmaker then sends to a volunteer a job description

Work After Work

provided by an organisation which has already filed details of a suitable job with the agency.

'Sometimes the volunteers need prodding,' says Nick Crace. 'They go off to Bermuda on a cruise in the middle of a job application! They may lose interest, or they may turn down six jobs in a row. It isn't easy to find a good match.'

People contact the agency either before retirement, or some time after when being at home is beginning to tell on them and their spouses. 'People hear of us from several sources,' says Mr Crace; 'from reference books, on the grapevine, from their old firms. We are becoming established now.'

Some placements are astoundingly successful, as in the case of the Guildford Red Cross director who wanted to stop work and found a replacement from a REACH recruit. Not only did the new director slip successfully into the director's role, he then promptly contacted REACH himself for some new 'staff'!

The major problem is geography. Where there may be jobs, there may not be any people wanting them or vice versa. Some counties, like Oxfordshire, have a balance of voluntary jobs and applicants but London suffers from the traditional exodus of retired people seeking more space. Charities tend to cluster in London, which would mean commuting all over again — not a pleasant prospect for someone just retired. REACH's deal with its volunteers is that the charity pays the volunteers' fare to work so groups are obviously keen to 'hire' executives within a ten-mile range of their offices. This can lead to frustration in job matching, because it reduces the number of volunteers available.

REACH's office in central London is a good example of a group practising what it preaches. Everyone working for the agency is a 'retired exec', except the director who is only fifty-five. Most of the staff were cleverly ensnared when applying for voluntary jobs themselves. 'It was fly in the spider's web stuff,' says Mr Crace. 'They would walk in unsuspecting, not realising that they were being sized up to work for REACH.'

The agency has three part-time matchmakers working three days a week each: an administration officer who services the matchmakers with the necessary files and computer information to help them make their matches; a business 'rep' who trawls the worlds of

Getting the Job

commerce and industry to inform them of REACH's services to their retiring staff — and also fund-raises to keep the office in business. There is also a press officer, who keeps REACH before the public eye both at national and local level.

Behind the scenes is a management council from business and voluntary organisations.

What are the jobs?

REACH matchmakers see life. In the piles of forms which constantly arrive on their desks there are many stories. Martin Brooks, one of the matchmakers, is amazed at the variety of unique groups operating in the United Kingdom, some only one-man-and-a-dog outfits, nevertheless helping someone, somewhere.

Martin is a former director of a Tarmac subsidiary, and before this he was with the United Africa Company, for thirty-six years. He is very glad to see the back of his executive days — 'all that jumping in and out of airplanes, rushing about. My wife tells me I'm much more reasonable to live with these days.'

Now Martin divides his time between REACH and the Small Firms Service of the Department of Industry where he is a counsellor. He has a much better time now, he says, than during his high-powered days. 'Although I'm still with Mammon the last two years have been the happiest of my life.'

At any time Martin has a large file of requests from groups for personnel, some professionally typed and accurately described, others sloppily handwritten and badly constructed. 'What they don't realise is that the volunteer is going to see these,' he says, 'and it won't do them any good at all.' A local scout council wants an administrator to be responsible for . . . Martin can't read it. 'Send it back,' he says with irritation. The International Society for Human Rights wants a translator and someone for publicity. . . . The Marriage Guidance Council wants a press officer too — retired journalists and PROs forward please . . . . The Working Ladies Guild is after a treasurer: 'We sent them a financial chap to sit on their committee, now they're after an honorary treasurer.' The Cam-

Work After Work

bridge Third World Education Group needs 'a resource person' — whatever that may be.

'Here's a good one: the Associates of the Victoria and Albert Museum want a company secretary with the additional role of overseeing accountancy. Two days a week, five hours a day, and possibly a long-term number. Nice job, I would have taken that myself.'

But Martin looks at all applicants as possibles, because even though one person looks good on paper, there may be others just as good.

A local council for voluntary service is explaining nervously that it hopes it can pay the volunteer's fare. 'Not a hope for them!' raps out Martin, 'our deal with our volunteers is — fares paid!'

The Society of Voluntary Associates wants three treasurers in different parts of London. Martin throws up his hands, 'Treasurers, accountants, book-keepers . . . where are they? Do they never retire?'

Charity shops are popping up everywhere and marketing beavers are needed. The Family Welfare Association wants an area trading co-ordinator. They know exactly what they want, which is a distinct advantage, but, as Martin knows too well, 'getting people to go to Dalston is the problem!'

An East End art project looks fascinating for someone with building or maintenance know-how. The project wants to convert a building into a studio for local artists, and negotiations have to be entered into with the borough's inspector. Perhaps a retired architect would suit here?

A cassette library for the blind and handicapped wants a manager for its computer department in Buckinghamshire. But the problem with high-tech requests is that the computer industry is so new that hardly anyone in it is of retiring age: the only hope is that computer operators would consider voluntary help — a tall order for some, but a computer hobbyist or two might come forward.

The Museum of Modern Art — 'No, not New York, unfortunately —' says Martin, has three jobs in Oxford: fund raiser, honorary secretary and librarian. 'I've just found a librarian in Oxford,' muses Martin. Matchmaking at REACH is a bit like playing the card game pelmanism!

Getting the Job

— Another treasurer is wanted for the National Association of Development Education Centres, and so NADEC joins the long list of people awaiting treasurers.

A high percentage of volunteers come back to the matchmaker with the cry 'this isn't right for me'. An inflexible attitude can sometimes be spotted in a volunteer which warns the matchmaker that success is going to be elusive.

— A Canals Trust wants an administrator and fund-raiser — someone with executive status who will co-ordinate its activities, which it says are the restoration of derelict local canals for the benefit of the community. Martin snorts: 'Nonsense, they want to do it for their own fun!' But the job seems an interesting one, with negotiations with local landowners a plus feature.

Accountants crop up continually in job requests. The British Atlantic Committee, an educational charity, wants someone to maintain day-to-day accounts, pay invoices, produce a monthly summary of accounts and prepare an annual audit. A community group catering for young people on two Pimlico estates wants something similar. The secretary has prepared the job request beautifully, describing the job in detail and bothering to paint a word picture of the lively club for children. 'This one will get a lot of attention from me,' promises Martin.

— The Clergy Orphan Corporation, caring for the fatherless children of the ordained, needs someone to reclaim tax on their behalf, collect investments, rents and handle legacies, for two-to-three days a week. A defined period of work each week is expected by REACH, but one self-help group for the disabled wriggles round it with the phrase 'at the volunteer's own time'. 'That's cowardly,' condemns Martin.

Who are the people?

Who are the job seekers who go to REACH? The variety is almost as wide as the jobs they chase. Some are at the end of their tether — bored and disenchanted with retirement; others have spotted this state of affairs in advance and are taking precautions. 'The demand for our services has hotted up almost beyond our capacity,' says

Work After Work

Martin Brooks. 'The good thing about REACH is that it is such a simple, straightforward idea which has identified its market, and is manageable.'

Martin has his own way of dealing with job hunters, which might vary from his two matchmaking colleagues Joan Simmons and Frances Bone — who also carries out REACH's research. 'I sort out the person who looks suitable for a job first, then I send them a copy of the organisation's job request form with a covering note. That eliminates the need for me to qualify the job description.'

Martin's people file is just as big as the jobs one. 'Here's a sixty-one-year-old lady who has been a lecturer and information expert. She would like to edit a small journal for someone or carry out secretarial or cataloguing work. I must find something to keep the grey matter turning over for this lady.'

— A sixty-one-year-old man from Hertfordshire who has spent thirty-one years as a cashier and buyer wants something within 10 miles of his home. Martin will have to do a persuading job to get him to travel further — plenty of groups further into London could use him. 'In the first flush of retirement they are the choosers,' he comments, knowing that time is his ally.

— A fifty-eight-year-old Birmingham metallurgist wants something two days a week. Says Martin, 'I'll have to use my imagination.'

— A retired army major who has experience of commerce as a sales manager could give marketing help to some organisation. He's a cinch!

— A former Fleet Air Arm engineer whose life has been airplanes: he wants to help the illiterate — ('he knows he's not going to be making any airplanes for anyone, sensible chap!') A van salesman says simply, 'I'll consider anything that needs effort.' This one might prove difficult, as will a seventy-six-year-old man who has been an accounts clerk: 'The age here is a problem. I'll just keep trying.'

— An ex-health authority engineer with know-how about installation and maintenance of, probably, large equipment: 'Another one for the imagination,' says Martin.

— A part-time teacher of primary children, aged fifty-seven, would like anything connected with crafts or artistic therapy. She

Getting the Job

makes an attractive plea that she wants to be an indian, not a chief. So what's the problem? 'It's East Anglia — there's damn little up there.'

— A shopkeeper aged sixty, who has 'kept books' for herself and her husband, writes simply that she wants something that will 'help people with any difficult area of their lives'. The couple are from Corby, 'the town that never gives up,' says Martin admiringly. 'It was severely shattered when the steel works closed, but people there are real fighters.'

— A forty-five-year-old chartered accountant — still working — offers some part time accountancy help. He's welcomed with open arms. Martin says he'll offer him to a big charity that needs top-class accountancy advice.

— A former managing director of a caravan firm, aged sixty-two, a founder member of the Social Democrat Party, follows country pursuits. He has 'little specific objective' other than a desire to help the unemployed or distressed, especially the young. 'I've spent twenty years in the higher reaches of administration,' he says, 'so I'm not an expert in anything.' Martin likes him for his honesty. 'He's not full of his own importance. There's good will here, and that's tremendous.'

— A fifty-four-year-old has been an office-boy-to-partner success story. He opened an antiques business when he retired, he has been an estate agent and will consider anything worthwhile that is interesting. He's a good all-rounder, which helps. The computer says he could be a tree-planter!

Martin has a headmaster to deal with. 'Now, how do you describe the attributes of head teachers, and what sort of work can I offer him?' Another one writes that he is prepared to consider anything, 'but like a lot of people, he doesn't mean it of course'.

— An ex-stockbroker and Foreign Office diplomat with overseas experience says he'll do general office duties in the SW1 area. Martin commends his 'no nonsense approach', but takes issue with the computer for suggesting a treasurer's job with the Citizens Advice Bureau: 'He hasn't got enough financial experience for that.'

— A workshop maintenance engineer might pose a problem with a request for meeting people and travelling. He makes the point on his form that he dislikes inefficiency. 'Shall I offer him a company

59

Work After Work

of scouts in Leicestershire?' debates Martin. However, difficult matches can take months, but the right jobs do occur, he assures us.

— A seventy-year-old former hotel manager and conference secretary has a sense of humour: he'll either organise an office, or be a dogsbody! ('There's flexibility for you.') An Abbeyfield home needs a catering adviser and these two look made for each other.

Even the titled apply to REACH: a sixty-two-year-old Baronet who has been a diplomatic and political correspondent, wants work. He could work for an organisation like Christian Aid or Oxfam who could use his contacts. He's even prepared to fund-raise.

Sometimes a REACH matchmaker will find an expert on a specific subject swimming into his net. But, although a highly desirable catch, he can give them problems in placing. Joan Simmons, who was the Tote personnel manager before joining REACH, recently found a man who dealt in social security benefits. He had been a DHSS regional social security manager and was up to date on thirty benefits to which people might be entitled, often without realising it. 'He insisted on using his experience, and I didn't want to waste him,' she says. She made a painstaking search and found an organisation dealing with the welfare of service families who jumped at the chance of using him.

Sometimes happily matched people phone in with thanks. Organisations usually get in touch to say thank you when they are ready to ask for someone else, but this is part of successful placing. In its own way REACH is pulling off some good social work: for one thing, saving marriages from the rocks of retirement. As Martin Brooks asks, acknowledging the sexism of his question, 'Who wants to be home when the hoover's going?'

In the market place

Selling a free service sounds a cushy job but, commercial wisdom being what it is, and the mentality of 'no such thing as a free service' widespread, REACH has to be marketed just like any other product.

REACH's full-time marketing director Robert Levene is a committed man. He sells REACH to industry with the conviction of a salesman introducing a brilliant new invention — which is exactly

Getting the Job

what he thinks it is. 'I'm sold on the value of REACH,' he says, 'and I'm determined to help it develop. It's choc-full of benefits and I can't think of a single negative aspect. It's of use to everyone and produces nothing but good. Even the most cynical are potential buyers.' There must be many commercial firms who would envy REACH's committed marketing man!

Robert finds REACH the easiest thing in the world to sell, once he gets past initial management disinterest. He has worked his way through *The Times* top 1,000 companies book, informing them of the service which can help their senior executives preparing for retirement. During the past three years he has visited nearly 400 companies spreading the REACH formula. At first he writes to chairmen — pointing out that he is a retired managing director himself — offering information to senior retiring employees. Then he visits the company. Sometimes the reaction is cold, and even hostile. One company chairman — the firm was 200 years old, employing 2,000 people — promptly indicated that his executives were too exhausted when they retired to do any voluntary work!

'Companies do feel sometimes that retirement is purely a matter for the individual to organise and they don't want anything to do with it,' he says. Robert has interviewed companies with an enlightened attitude to human relations who show concern for retiring staff but there are many — even large companies — whose lack of pre-retirement planning reflects a generally uncaring policy.

Robert's approach to industry is founded on twenty-seven years' experience with the famous sales training organisation Tack Training International. Robert was managing director of three of the organisation's firms dealing with research, publications and management consultancy, and an instructor in marketing and selling. 'Selling is a mental thing,' he says. 'You don't sell a washing machine, you sell freedom from chores. You are imparting a mental message, because selling is based on benefits, and I'm selling a beneficial concept in REACH. I hope my belief and faith come over to people.'

Some firms have spotted the value of REACH and spread the word to their staff. Robert backs this up by feeding back to managers details of their employees who have been successfully matched. Other companies agree to take brochures but then fail to

Work After Work

promote the literature. 'The brochures find their way into personnel departments who regard them as just another piece of paper to deal with. The message doesn't get much further on in this kind of situation,' says Robert. Nonetheless, he doesn't have an aggressive line in fund raising. If firms want to make a donation, he's delighted, and they often do. But he does not tout for money. 'I never discuss it but if people ask me where we get our money from I tell them how we are funded. Sometimes management will tell us they have a charity budget and might make a donation from that.' Later on in the relationship Robert will write a letter appealing for funds. 'Some firms are cold towards us but most see us as worthwhile,' he says.

Robert carries on 'converting', the mark of a true salesman.

One indication that his dedication paid off came when three managing directors — all from companies who did not avail themselves of the agency's services — contacted him when their own retirement loomed. 'A pity they didn't share the message with their staff,' says Robert.

Read all about it!

Good news is usually bad news for newspapers. Most news editors know that readers go straight for the scandalous stories, and those papers who have experimented with 'good news columns' have caught a cold — nobody reads them. But REACH appeals to journalists for its simple, straightforward message. Here is a good news story that catches the eye.

REACH's press officer, Ralph Allman, himself a provincial paper journalist for thirty years, tempts local, regional and national newspapers, radio and TV, with snippets from REACH's workload. Many catch the bait and the agency is beginning to get publicity on a nationwide basis. 'REACH can only go on expanding by being better known. We need more volunteers coming forward, particularly regionally,' he says. 'There are more jobs than people in some areas — like Greater London with 352 jobs wanting people and only 94 volunteers.'

Although the agency's director wanted national publicity, Ralph

Getting the Job

wanted to concentrate at first on local newspapers so that the 'problem' areas could be stimulated into producing more volunteers. Ralph knows many newspaper editors from his years as deputy director of the National Council for the Training of Journalists. He has sent 'letters to the editor' to papers all over the country, which are usually picked up for their story value by alert news editors or reporters. Ralph scours the REACH matchmakers' files to find stories tailored to local areas, which is what the weeklies want. Local radio and regional TV stations pick up stories from REACH and the agency's director finds himself interviewed regularly. Slowly, the idea of voluntary work for retired executives is reaching its targets, the men and women about to give up salaried employment.

Ralph is concentrating on areas like the West Midlands and the South East where the matchmakers tell him they need more people. 'People read local papers,' he insists. 'Radio and TV are fine but they have got to be looked at and listened to, whereas the paper can be read any time during the week. Local papers are a habit people acquire.'

Company house journals are now coming into the trawl, as they are a good showplace for pre-retirement staff. Ralph is methodically working through all media possibilities. He started in journalism as a copy boy in the sub-editors' room of the *Birmingham Evening Mail* and rose to be features editor of the *Wolverhampton Express and Star*, and later editor of the *West Country Sunday Independent*. As a retired journalist he is now a good example of the REACH philosophy — he is publicity officer for his local Multiple Sclerosis Society branch and volunteer for the local Victim Support Scheme, as well as putting REACH on the media map.

Retired journalists are in short supply for voluntary jobs, 'probably because there are less of them than other groups,' says Ralph. But REACH could certainly use more news and features writers and broadcasters to help charities — like itself — spread their message.

Sometimes one story goes a long way: many 'letters to the editor' might stay ignored on desks but an article in a national newspaper will revive everyone's interest. A piece in the *Standard* was picked up enthusiastically by local papers wanting to know if REACH had made any placements in their patch.

Work After Work

'It is a good story basically,' says Ralph, 'but we have to catch people's attention with what we can. We can't compete with bomb explosions and bank robberies in the news, but there are many parts of a newspaper not directly connected to instant news — like social, environmental and educational fields — which we can aim for. We are even trying to write up the annual report as a news story. These reports can be very dull if you don't do anything with them.'

To sum up, REACH gets into print where it can, but it can be hit-and-miss. 'You can plan something in detail,' warns Ralph, 'but it doesn't mean you'll get publicity.'

Volunteer bureaux

Not everyone wants to specialise after retirement. Further executive responsibility may seem less than alluring and getting out into the field as a volunteer could be an ideal antidote to a sedentary career. At least it could provide a period of reflection in which direct contact with clients will show the extent of their problems.

As a 'non-executive' volunteer you could find yourself face to face with some distressing personal situations, but the rewards can be satisfying if you find you have helped someone significantly. There are many people at home or in hospital in your locality who through disability lead restricted lives. The companionship and practical help of volunteers can transform their dull existence.

The best way to approach a field job is through a volunteer bureau. These are often set up by Councils for Voluntary Service, groups trying to extend local voluntary action at all levels. The bureaux have job shops, advertise in local papers, publicise their work in factories and through personnel departments. They have recruitment drives in shopping centres, circulate beer mats with a message, put posters on buses and in launderettes in order to reach those people unfamiliar with volunteering. If all this has passed you by before, the local bureau will happily fill you in on what voluntary work is available in your area. There are 250 of them, and a directory can be bought from the Volunteer Centre in Berkhamsted. The Centre also has an information service.

Volunteers often give the bureaux ideas for local initiatives.

Getting the Job

Musically talented volunteers have started classes for handicapped adults in hospitals or day centres and those who have dabbled in amateur dramatics have used this to entertain both young and old in and out of hospital.

Staff at bureaux do not merely set the volunteer up in 'work' and then disappear. They are eager for feedback and often monitor progress, if only to see that the volunteer doesn't become disenchanted. They keep in touch with the bureau customers, such as hospitals and some statutory departments like social services, to see that the jobs are imaginatively deployed.

The staff support volunteers if problems arise, which they do, of course. One bureau found that its volunteers were only lasting a few weeks at a local hospital and it investigated to find that the jobs had not been thought through properly and the paid staff had not been sufficiently briefed about the volunteers, who were left to manage on their own initiative. The bureau pulled out its volunteers and later, after negotiation with the medical staff, a hospital co-ordinator was hired.

Some bureaux use job description forms to make sure that agencies needing their volunteers are going to use them in appropriate ways. Experience has taught them that this is wise. In one case a bureau had to point out to a geriatric hospital that carrying out dead patients was not a proper function for a volunteer.

Proper payment of expenses should be part of the voluntary deal and the bureau will often take up the cudgels on your behalf if the amount reimbursed for fares or other expenditure you are involved in is not adequate — or is not being paid when it should.

Bureaux also talk through problems with trades unions about where a volunteer can be used without crossing the paid work line, especially during disputes.

Swindon volunteer bureau is a good example of how the system works. The bureau sees an average of 400 volunteers a year and places the majority of them — last year only fifteen people were not fixed up. A cross-section of the local population apply for voluntary work, from teenagers to the over-sixties, and they vary from manual workers, married women who do not have jobs outside the home, the unemployed and some retired workers. The bureau does not see many senior executives.

Work After Work

Like most bureaux, Swindon has trouble finding treasurers. Not just bookkeeping skills are in demand but help with budgeting, grants and planning is needed badly.

The bureau has about eighty different job titles, and it has a good selection of voluntary groups locally and regionally to serve. The jobs range across helping on an individual level: visiting the elderly; youth counselling; befriending those who have been mentally ill. They also undertake group help: playgroup helpers; visiting geriatric or mental handicap wards to play cards or other games with patients; meals on wheels driving; adult literacy classes; assisting at hydrotherapy sessions.

The bureau is careful not to find jobs for the unemployed which require befriending skills, in case the volunteer is fortunate enough to find a job and may then have to break the relationship. The unemployed are more likely to be offered meals on wheels driving which is less personal than visiting elderly people for companionship.

Swindon does admit there are problems with the payment of expenses sometimes, if the voluntary group is very short of funds. 'The bureau makes a particular point of always covering travelling expenses itself so that we can encourage others to do the same,' says organiser Glenys Baker. 'We think this is important for unemployed volunteers.' Volunteers tend to conform to a pattern, she says: 'They either give up quickly, or they stay in the jobs for a long time.'

Once you have taken a job locally you will see how much unmet need there is in your neighbourhood and you may then be in a position to suggest further work for yourself or others. As the Volunteer Centre points out, it was the initiative of a volunteer who started the rural prescription collection service which is now such a boon to housebound patients.

If you felt strongly enough, you could start your own voluntary bureau — more are always needed because in areas where there are no 'go-betweens' it is much more difficult for people to find the voluntary job which is exactly right for them. A number of local organisations like Community Health Councils, Rural Community Councils, Citizens' Advice Bureaux and the Social Services area director will help in outlining the kind of agencies which need

Getting the Job

voluntary help. There is a special unit at the Volunteer Centre to help people bold enough to take on this kind of venture.

RICHARD WRIGHT

Age 64
Previous occupation Cost surveyor and materials controller with a construction company.
Occupation now Administering the affairs of the Leighton Buzzard Narrow Gauge Railway. The railway runs in the summer and carries on average 10,000 paying passengers a year. Last year the railway journey of just under two miles was extended to three by an ambitious project helped by the Youth Opportunities Scheme at a cost of £8,000.

The railway is run by a 240-strong group of rail enthusiasts who have kept the steam locos moving since British Rail closed the line in 1969. Originally the narrow gauge rail had been used to transport sand from a local quarry to a loading bay. The society has half a dozen steam engines with delightful names like Pixie and Elf, and a collection of fourteen diesels.

The line is managed by the volunteer members, who restore the engines, build new coaches for passengers, run a buffet and a souvenir shop. As they are all in jobs as well, such as commercial artists, bank employees and civil engineers, they were anxious to find an administrator who could pull the whole operation together. Richard Wright takes up the story:

'We spent the winter relaying the abandoned stretch of track with the help of twelve boys and two full-time supervisors under the old Youth Opportunities Scheme. We paid the supervisors' salary and then recovered it from the Manpower Services Commission. We taught the boys how to drive diesel locos and to use acetylene burners. They clamoured to drive and we had to ration the driving!

'I had to make sure it was safe for them too as we were relaying tracks across a public road. We run across five public

Work After Work

roads on our trips and we have flagmen who jump down from the train and check it is safe to go across. We don't hold anyone up really, just a couple of cars, the occasional lorry, because mostly we only open on Sundays and Bank holidays.

'Because we run on a two-foot rail we can't buy materials so we have to build our own coaches, finding cheap materials where we can. It's all voluntary labour — just people interested in locos. The head of the steam loco department is a tinplate worker, and we have a couple of British Rail employees in the membership to help us keep on the right side of the regulations.

'Coaches take about 12 months to make from scratch and we paint them to make them waterproof. One of our engines — it's 105 years old — has been on display at the railway museum in York.

'I have a multitude of jobs as administrator. I keep the souvenir shop stocked up, and I am seeking voluntary help from scouts, guides and schoolchildren to help us run the buffet through the summer season. I'm searching for advertisers for a new guide book, and I'm trying to persuade coach operators within a 100 mile radius to include us in some of their tours.

'We put our diesel engines on show and use them occasionally but being hauled by steam is the main attraction. We attract about 400 people a day at the height of the season.

'I didn't know a thing about railways when I retired. But I'm learning fast and I have caught the enthusiasm of my colleagues in the society. I'm very happy in this job and I hope to stay.'

Comment from the society's chairman Arthur Fisher: 'We've had a tremendous year relaying the abandoned mile of track with a little grant from the council and help from the MSC and we couldn't have done it without our administrator. He's fantastic.'

Getting the Job

Richard Wright with Elf, a loco which spent its working life in the French Cameroons and came to Britain in 1973, now in service on the Leighton Buzzard Narrow Gauge Railway. Picture by Derek Smith.

Useful addresses
REACH, Victoria House, Southampton Row, London WC1. Tel. 01-404 0940
Volunteer Centre 29 Lower Kings Road, Berkhamsted, Herts HP4 2AB. Tel. 04427-73311.

CHAPTER FIVE

SO YOU STILL WANT MONEY?

The habit of working for money dies hard. You may be finished with the nine-to-five (or round-the-clock) routine but remain committed to the need, or the desire, to earn money. People who have been used to providing their services for a fee or salary somehow find that the act of removing payment reduces the value of their work. Psychologically, if not economically, the money is important.

This particular problem is taxing Stephen O'Brien of Business in the Community. He suspects that real commitment doesn't come without pay. There are instances of community projects running aground because an unpaid worker has not put in an appropriate amount of time. 'Some charities wouldn't survive without proper discipline,' he says. 'That is terribly difficult to maintain if people are giving their time freely. You have no real control over them without some fee or payment.' Obviously he is beginning to consider the possibility of paid 'volunteers'.

At Action Resource Centre full-time managers are paid, and they are often former business personnel who have retired early. 'We employ managers in areas where we have been funded,' says Cecilia Allen. 'We need the commitment. It is very unsettling for staff to have a manager change every so often, so we prefer full-time people.

'They come from a wide variety of backgrounds, often from large firms. A lot of people write to us — quite high-powered people — and we do what we can to employ them.'

Payment would, of course, mean that you would be deferring retirement. And the problem for most voluntary bodies is that they operate on a shoestring anyway. As Nick Crace of REACH says, 'What happens if the organisation you actually want to work for can't afford to pay you?'

So You Still Want Money?

After retirement or redundancy late in life, what are the prospects of continuing to work for pay? Slim. But there are ways of chasing jobs when you are fifty-plus and in a recession. Success After Sixty is a commercial but non-profitmaking job-finding agency which is part of Career Care Group Holdings, a large specialist employment agency dealing in accountancy and banking personnel. It was created in 1975 by a successful businessman, Richard Broyd, who ran Accountancy Personnel.

Broyd saw that older people with a wealth of experience were passed by in the job market. Success After Sixty charges the employer a lower fee than average, and the rest of the group subsidises the agency. Like everyone else, it has been hit by the recession and two branches, at Slough and Manchester, have had to close because of the dearth of jobs in those areas. 'In 1975 you could place a seventy-year-old,' says Bill Piggott, manager of the agency's Bond Street branch, 'now that's impossible. It is an employer's market.'

Even so, Success After Sixty can place two out of five applicants. It deals almost exclusively with office work — anything from accountants to tea ladies and cleaners. The trend in vacancies now seems to be for accountancy-related jobs whereas two years ago filing, clerking and messenger jobs were easier to get.

The agency helps people aged from fifty onwards, despite its name. Executives who have been earning in the £15,000–£20,000 bracket go to it happy to accept jobs like post clerk. 'The majority of people want something lighter when they retire,' says Mr Piggott, 'they've had all the pressure of a prestige job and are happy to take on something with little responsibility. They only want to be occupied and be out during the day.

'Retirement can cause problems at home when a wife, who isn't retiring, has an organised life and suddenly finds her husband in the way. It can happen however happy a couple are.'

Although former executives are pleased to take on low-profile jobs, prospective employers find it hard to swallow. 'When they realise that the applicant for their filing clerk's job was a financial director or a sales manager they fear that he will not want to do such a mundane task,' says Mr Piggott.

People who are not really worried about the money — usually

Work After Work

those retiring on target — are sometimes directed to REACH. The real problem job hunters are those unfortunate enough to be made redundant at around fifty-five. 'If it is a man who has been earning £15,000 his whole future has been built on the assumption that he will be going on until sixty-five on an increasing salary. He will probably have a house in the stockbroker belt and have a couple of children at boarding school. He has really got a problem.

'He comes in still looking for a £15,000 salary because of his commitments. He is just not going to get it. Although I don't have this problem, I am sixty-six years old and I'm able to talk sympathetically to them and I gradually get them to look at the situation more realistically. They have got to reassess their whole life and they will have to cut back and learn to manage on perhaps half their last salary.' Bill Piggott feels that although the last two years have been 'difficult' for fifty-plus job-hunters, 'there are slight signs of improvement'.

The past two years have seen the growth of a self-help movement which began in the North of England but is now catching on countrywide. Groups are formed on the assumption that it is better to tackle joblessness in numbers, for mutual support and stimulation of ideas in the hunt for work.

In the managerial and professional field EXACT — Executives in Action — helps retired or redundant executives to find jobs or to start their own business. EXACT is the brain child of the Rotary movement. In 1980 Nottingham and Ilkley Rotary had the idea simultaneously. In Ilkley chemist Brian Jackson was disturbed to find some of his regular customers becoming introverted and depressed. 'In every case I'd find out that they had lost their jobs or retired. They were confident people who gradually became shadows,' he recalls, 'and I thought how lucky I was being self-employed.'

Ilkley is a commuter town a few miles from Leeds and Bradford. Local unemployment is made up of managerial and professional people — particularly lecturers suffering from educational cutbacks. 'These are the people who could help themselves,' says Mr Jackson, 'so we decided to start a self-help group.'

EXACT groups meet regularly and make sure local employers are fully aware of their existence, and jobs are offered to members.

So You Still Want Money?

As more groups spring up — in mid 1983 there were twenty branches — the membership becomes more positive, with approaches made to employers. Often members are tempted into self-employment by the encouragement of fellow members.

One man in the Ilkley branch felt he was on the scrapheap when he left his brother's firm after a boardroom squabble. He was part Spanish, with a Spanish name, and felt this was preventing him getting a job. 'He heard about EXACT and came along to a meeting,' says Mr Jackson. 'He was very depressed and felt he had no future. But later on he started to pep up at meetings and contributed instead of moaning all the time. That's when people start getting better. I told him he had a lot going for him — even with his Spanish name. Now he has his own business — importing Spanish wines!'

Other EXACT members might want to branch out on their own in their own speciality but are worried about their lack of business organisation. This is where other members, who may have the missing expertise, come in. Such groups are being formed all the time and the best way to find out if there is one near you is to contact the local Rotary District Officer.

Although job-hunting for the fifty-plus is a nightmare, self-employment is becoming a more attractive proposition. A number of initiatives, both private and government, have been set up to advise and help those people who want to have a go. Stephen O'Brien's organisation Business in the Community is responsible for starting local Enterprise Agencies which exist to help small businesses get going, or to improve those already in existence. 'Small business' can mean just you on your own. The agencies, which are popping up everywhere (see the list of them on page 143), have a director and secretary each and they offer advice on premises — and a lot of other matters besides — to those wanting to set up on their own. The London Enterprise Agency has helped set up over 140 small firms, creating 2,000 jobs.

The Department of Industry runs the Small Firms Service which has a network of counsellors ready to advise people wanting to begin their own enterprise, or to help those small firms already in existence. Counsellors help with a range of advice, from organisation to sales and marketing, from manufacturing to shopkeeping.

Work After Work

The service does not help financially but the DoI does operate, in conjunction with the banks, the Loan Guarantee Scheme. The scheme guarantees 80% of a loan without security, up to a maximum of £75,000. The Small Firms Service can be reached by asking the operator for Freefone 2444.

The 1983 Budget extended the Enterprise Allowance Scheme to the whole country. Originally this only operated in Medway, Coventry, North-East Lancashire, North Wales and North Ayrshire. People with a good idea for a business — mainly for their own employment — can apply to the Scheme. If they can successfully persuade officers of the Manpower Services Commission, which has £50 million to fuel the scheme, that they qualify under the scheme, they will be paid a weekly taxable allowance of £40 for a year to start their business. Applicants must be able to show they have at least £1,000 to put into the business. They must be between the ages of eighteen and State retirement age, and they must have been unemployed for 13 weeks, or be receiving social security benefit. You will qualify for this if you are formally under notice of redundancy or have been made redundant below the age of sixty-five, for a man, and sixty for a woman. But compulsory or voluntary retirement disqualifies. The scheme is aimed at promoting small-scale self-employment and the DoI Small Firms Service counsellors provide the necessary back up advice to successful candidates.

What are the chances of a successful application? From 1 August 1983 until March 1984 — but there is to be an extension — there have been 25,000 available places under the scheme. These are mostly allocated in line with areas of high unemployment. In the first year of the scheme, ending February 1983, 3,590 people applied and 2,319 were successful. No industries are excluded although officers judging applicants have to bear in mind what is a suitable venture to attract public funds. This scheme may be one way of discouraging working while collecting unemployment benefit but it would be a heaven-sent opportunity for a late-fifties redundant executive to try self-employment.

The scheme is being operated mainly through Job Centres.

One man who turned his own retirement into a thriving business is Tony Timbs, a former lecturer at a Southampton college of higher education. Tony gave short courses on retirement to industry until

So You Still Want Money?

education cuts brought them to a halt. But he was continually approached and asked 'when are you going to run another course?' So when Tony retired in 1982 he set up New Life Retirement Service. 'I thought hard about it for a year,' he says. 'I sent questionnaires to firms to see if they would be interested for their retiring staff and I was encouraged by their replies.'

Tony's service appeals mostly to the smaller firm with no full-time personnel department. His courses are packed with information on every benefit available to the retired, from entertainment and travel concessions — 'most people don't know they can take the car over the channel at half the price with some ferry companies if they belong to their share-owning schemes' — to adult education possibilities.

He also goes into the possibilities of self-employment and running small businesses. 'On one of my courses there were some TV South cameramen who were retiring early and they were interested in how I had set up my business. They wanted something to do between fifty-eight and the State retirement age, so I documented all the steps I took and incorporated it into the curriculum.

'If you want a part-time job you are better employing your own skill. Apart from lollipop men and women there seem to be few permanent jobs for the retired.'

Tony's courses are held in the Chamber of Commerce, and he will hold them on a firm's premises if there are enough staff retiring.

'I work at it steadily,' he says. 'If I don't want to do any work on it, I don't. But if the weather is wet, or the garden or golf seem unattractive, I do some work on it.'

Tony is working with a young freelance copywriter to improve the service's image and its publicity. There are plans for expansion — 'but I have to make sure my marketing is right. Like many small businesses people are often interested in the beginning, but you have to sustain their custom.' What Tony needs is a partner, 'someone who will come in with me, who can handle the business side. I take care of the teaching side but I need someone who will approach firms for custom — you know, the foot in the door stuff. I know I have a good product but I need to sell it.'

One way to test your inclination to self-employment would be to buy a copy of the 'Be Your Own Boss' kit, developed by the

Work After Work

National Extension College to link in with the Yorkshire television series. The kit helps you decide on a number of things: whether self-employment is the right answer for you; whether you have the capacity; if the business you have in mind stands a chance; and it also gives practical advice on money, taxation, location, marketing and planning. The kit can be ordered by post from the National Extension College, 18 Brooklands Avenue, Cambridge CB2 2HN. It costs £5.95, including postage.

Benefiting from savings

Your savings can bring you an income. But the savings and investment market is a stormy sea of brokers and salesmen with conflicting advice, and if your business career has not called for financial expertise you may wonder what to do with your savings. To start with, there are a couple of 'don'ts' about dealing with money.

Tom Tickell, a financial journalist, is deputy city editor of the *Mail on Sunday*. Tom's guidelines are simple: don't believe salesmen, they only deal in half-truths; don't put money in a building society if you don't pay tax; don't commit your money for too long a period if you have very little; and don't take risks unless you can afford to write them off to experience. 'The pleasures of doing well are nothing compared to the horrors of losing your savings,' warns Tom. 'Avoid people who say they have the answer, fast talkers with no-risk promises. They are conmen.' If you have around £30,000 it is better to seek advice. Up to £6,000 and you can do-it-yourself.

'But the crucial thing to remember,' says Tom, 'is that everyone has an axe to grind. The bank manager will want to sell you unit trusts. An insurance salesman will want to flog insurance contracts.'

There is a variety of ways to draw income from savings. There are term shares (building societies), National Savings Income Bonds, local authority bonds, and in the longer term savings field there are the famous granny bonds (now open to savers of any age), National Savings Certificates, and inflation-proofed gilts. Redundancy money, or a part of a pension, can be channelled into the National Savings Income Bonds. This way you can receive a monthly amount of interest into your bank, but you cannot pull money out

So You Still Want Money?

immediately, which is the main problem with schemes bearing attractive interest rates.

You can loan money to local authorities to help them with their building projects. Interest rates are fixed with these bonds, and the councils pay out twice a year by cheque. They pay the tax first and if you don't pay tax you can get it back from your tax office. These bonds have been a good idea for the retired because the tax can be reclaimed, but again you have to tie the money up, usually for several years.

By the time you retire you will no doubt have your pension sewn up. Steps to take one out or to improve an existing one can be taken years before retirement. If you have been self-employed it makes sense to take one out as tax relief — at top rate — means that a contribution of £1,000 actually costs £500.

Self-employment pensions will usually allow you to vary yearly contributions, in case income fluctuates. Of course, the later you leave it, the less time the pension has to grow. It doesn't make sense taking one out in the late fifties or early sixties.

But there is a step you can take in your fifties to improve the pension you receive later. There are some snags and limitations, but if you can arrange it you will benefit. Additional Voluntary Contributions — AVCs — will enlarge your pension. Payments can be set off against tax and they go into a fund which gives tax-free interest. You collect on retirement a tax-free cheque. The problem with this is, again, having the money tied-up and inaccessible, and not every firm can operate the scheme. The AVC scheme can only be arranged through a company with a contracted-out pension plan — those relying on the State scheme cannot fix it up for you. The trustees of the company's pension plan will arrange AVCs, and there are limits to the amount you contribute. Even so, this pension-boost is well worth considering in the pre-retirement years.

Tom Tickell has written a booklet explaining — and simply — many of the options open for savings and it can be picked up in branches of the Halifax Building Society. It is called *The Savings Market and You*.

Work After Work

FREDERICK and DORIS WATTS

Ages Early seventies.
Previous occupations Mr Watts was a Principal Scientific Officer in the civil service for thirty years, and is a Fellow of the Royal Statistical Society. Mrs Watts was a school secretary.
Occupations now Mr Watts is an archivist at the Tank Museum, Bovington Camp, Wareham in Dorset and Mrs Watts helps with administration in the museum office. According to Mrs Watts, her husband is happiest when he is debuging a computer programme.

The Tank Museum has a photographic collection which claims a picture of every armoured vehicle in the world. It also contains the archives of the Royal Tank Regiment and the Royal Armoured Corps, and 'the job of indexing this enormous amount of paper will see me out', says Mr Watts. 'This is very important and urgent work but it is grotesque in its magnitude! The information is lying on shelves and the indexation is not very effective. There hasn't been a real attempt to index it and it'll take three lifetimes to get into order.

'My wife and I work here two days a week but I would really like to be working the whole week. I never really retired, although I 'officially' retired four times. At sixty, instead of leaving I was demoted to a research grade from a scientific post. Then at sixty-three I left that job and became a data processing clerk for a financial company. At sixty-five I left and became a librarian for six years. Now I'm sorting out the files of the Tank Museum. It's quite a long way from where we live but we share the driving and the Museum gives us a petrol allowance.'

Lieutenant Colonel George Forty, the museum's curator, says he is 'tickled pink' with his two volunteers. 'She's an ace typist and whistles through a lot of the office work and he is marvellous at sorting out the major collections we have.'

So You Still Want Money?

Frank Watts at work in the Tank Museum.

Useful addresses
Success After Sixty 40/41 Old Bond Street, London W1. Tel. 01-629 0672 and 33 George Street, Croydon. Tel. 01-680 0858.
Small Firms Service, Freefone 2444.
New Life Retirement Service Dolphin Field, Roman Road, Winchester, Hants. Tel. 0962-712014.

CHAPTER SIX

TOP TEN

Once you get into a charity there are various views about how you can help best. You can just get on with your work as you have always done — a course much recommended by Nick Crace at REACH, who views an over-emotional involvement with the aims of the new 'boss' as distracting and dangerous. 'If volunteers get too fired with enthusiasm they may start taking over,' he warns. But others may think the 'perks' of the job would be the amount of enthusiasm felt for the ideals of the organisation. General Bob Loudoun of the Mental Health Foundation thinks that new volunteers must be wholeheartedly behind the aims of the group, and this, he believes, is where job satisfaction comes in.

Obviously, idealism has to be handled with care. You may admire the group you go to work for but you can't abandon structure for idealism, otherwise the skills you bring from your working life — the very reason you are needed — will be wasted.

But idealism may be the point of entry for you. Are you aware that thousands of voluntary organisations exist in Britain covering every aspect of human endeavour and need? A glance through a classified list (see page 130) would surprise you by the sheer breadth of coverage it shows. More groups are constantly springing up, dealing with needs as they become apparent. So here are potted outlines of ten of the leading grant-seeking charities, starting with:

Oxfam

This giant of the Third World had humble beginnings. The first money raised — £3,200 — helped children in occupied Greece in 1943. More cash was raised but the government stepped in and prevented it going abroad in case it inadvertently helped the Germans. One of the first 'public controversies' over foreign aid erupted after this decision! Thousands of people protested at the government although its decision remained. But a point had been made — that human need over-rode political considerations.

After the war Oxfam began a method of working which it has stayed faithful to ever since. Money and clothes are sent to local workers where disasters occur, rather than Oxfam masterminding its programme from home.

The war had been the stimulus for Oxfam's help, and as the European picture lightened, Oxfam thought its work might be over, but the charity did not have to wait long to see that it would be permanently needed. In 1949 the Palestinian refugees made their first appearance and Oxfam defined its aim: 'The relief of suffering arising out of war or any other cause in any part of the world.'

In the early fifties Oxfam dealt more in clothes than money. It ran a small paid staff, and in 1949–50 its budget was £100,000. By the end of the decade that had leapt to £1 million. By this time Oxfam used regional organisers who were responsible for local collections of money and clothing.

Oxfam has been there during all the major natural and man-made disasters of the last thirty years: 1950 Korean war, 1956 Hungarian uprising, 1957 Algerian war, 1960 Congo civil war, Nigerian/Biafran war. Oxfam drew attention to what was going on in Kampuchea in 1979.

During this time the natural disasters have included drought, earthquake, famine, cyclone — and even flooding back home. Wherever there has been a massive tragedy which has thrown refugees onto the mercy of the rest of the world, Oxfam has been there.

No voluntary organisation involved in famine relief stays the same for long; soon enough the realisation dawns that symptom-relief is useless and long-term help is needed for the poorest regions of the world. In the sixties Oxfam turned into a development agency, at first contributing to 400 projects in Asia, Africa and the Middle

Work After Work

East which were designed to help local populations improve their food production.

There were well over 1,000 overseas projects being supported by Oxfam in 1981/2, in the areas of health, social development and agriculture. Oxfam's first overseas representative had been appointed in 1962; now there are 25 field offices recruiting local staff. Out in the field, volunteers learned a great deal about poverty and its causes, so Oxfam began a programme to filter this knowledge to people at home. An agreement was reached in 1974 to spend 5 per cent of its income on home-based education. Just asking people for donations without spelling out why the money was needed seemed patronising, so Oxfam now has an education department and a public affairs unit to provide research, and materials for schools.

To support all this work overseas, Oxfam has had to do some energetic capital-raising in the United Kingdom. In 1965 there were 400 groups being co-ordinated by twenty regional organisers and a trading company called Oxfam Activities was set up, dealing in the Christmas card, tea towel and handicrafts business. This company was soon importing from the countries it was seeking to help, giving them an extra boost. The local groups threw themselves into sponsored walks, collections and selling publicly-donated goods. By 1969 the Oxfam budget had shot up to £$3\frac{1}{4}$ million. In 1980 donations to Oxfam reached £$18\frac{3}{4}$ million.

The past ten years has seen a streamlining of the local shops, with better gifts on sale, so that marketing has become all-important. New shops have continually opened so that they now number 620. Oxfam also has a recycling plant in Huddersfield dealing with textiles and aluminium, which is another attempt to spotlight the world's dwindling energy resources. The charity is continually gaining in technical expertise, and has helped develop a series of emergency kits to cover sanitation, water supply, shelters and feeding to use during disasters.

The aim for the eighties is to increase the British public's — and government's — awareness of the problems of poor countries, and how they impinge on our own welfare. Oxfam is actively recruiting more volunteers and supporters, encouraging more people to visit its headquarters to see what is going on.

Top Ten

Oxfam's central donor register, bearing 270,000 names, has been computerised and this technology has been put to use by the charity's trading company and overseas division.

The charity has produced a leaflet called 'Links In The Chain' which lists jobs for volunteers.

As part of its campaign to show work to the public, Oxfam has distributed more than 20,000 copies of its study pack on the Brandt report *North–South: a Programme for Survival.*

The range of help to developing countries is astonishing. Between May 1981 and April 1982 Oxfam spent £10.2 million abroad and here are just a few examples of where the money went:

Bangladesh: Jessore literacy programme, teachers' salaries, rent and teaching materials — £6,831.

Bhutan: ambulances and materials for rural dispensaries — £8,370.

Brazil: horses' harness and plough for two communal agricultural groups — £405; setting up crude rubber and nut marketing co-op — £1,397.

Burundi: tools for carpentry training — £1,510.

Colombia: Bogota, medical staff salaries, supplies and equipment for slum health programme — £19,787.

Djibouti (with Catholic Relief Services): Construction of dam for irrigation and cattle — £10,000.

El Salvador (in conjunction with local church group): food and equipment for displaced people — £106,382.

Italy: temporary community centre for earthquake victims — £15,000.

Kampuchea (with other voluntary agencies): fertiliser and seeds for Kompong Speu province — £165,925.

Lebanon: repairs and equipment for St Luke's Home for the Mentally Retarded — £12,000.

South Africa: North Transvaal, supplies for malnourished children — £1,340.

Uganda: Kapedo Se Settlement Scheme, salaries, farming equipment, building materials, agricultural input — £73,386.

To help Oxfam is to broaden your conception of the rest of the world. The Brandt report tried to show the vast gulf of misunderstanding between the rich northern countries and the poor

South. As the report said, 'the idea of a community of nations has little meaning . . . if hunger is regarded as a marginal problem which humanity can live with.'

Cancer Research Campaign
and
Imperial Cancer Research Fund

Cancer conquest is in the forefront of UK charities. Two research organisations, the Cancer Research Campaign and the Imperial Cancer Research Fund occupy the second and third position in the top 200 grant-seeking charities league. These two major voluntary organisations are committed to pouring funds into the many research projects in hospitals, clinics, universities and laboratories throughout the country. The Imperial Fund pays for work at its own laboratories and the Campaign funds research in other people's laboratories — in teaching hospitals and universities.

Cancer still freezes the public's imagination, but much headway has been made. Although given one name, it is really an umbrella term for more than 200 malignant diseases. There has been more success in treating some than others. The statistics are still fairly appalling, with a yearly death rate in the United Kingdom of more than 145,000. One out of every three people are expected to develop a cancer, and one out of five will die.

The controversy surrounding lung cancer's connection with smoking is beginning to benefit men — but not women. Men are starting to put out their cigarettes, which is not surprising as male lung cancer deaths accounted for 40 per cent of total cancer mortality in men. The Cancer Research Campaign points out that this disease was once extremely rare, for it was nearly 300 years before cigarettes replaced tobacco-filled pipes and snuff in this country. The First World War saw the population lighting up in ever increasing numbers — a national habit was being formed. Taking the long incubation period as twenty years, those picking up the

Top Ten

habit in the 1920s were becoming the mortality statistics of the 1940s and 1950s.

Women were slower in taking to cigarettes but are now smoking more. As men kick the habit, women pick it up — and we are seeing their lung cancer rates rising. The Campaign is putting money into educational programmes aimed at giving the public — particularly the young — the full facts about smoking, so that freedom of choice in deciding to smoke or not can be made in awareness. But there are still large numbers of people ignorant of the dangers.

The Cancer Research Campaign gives grants to medical schools and institutes, and its own laboratory at Mount Vernon hospital. Although the main target is research, great importance is placed on improving care for patients.

Because cancer is not one illness with one cause to discover, research covers a multitude of fields. The Campaign has set up some intensive research groups of scientists looking at cancer-causing substances and how the body deals with them; life-style and diet; and how to lessen the damage to normal tissue from radiation during therapy. Funds also go towards expensive equipment like body scanners, fluorescent activated cell sorters, cyclotron for radiotherapy, and a linear accelerator.

The Campaign is also supporting an investigation into the causes of childhood cancer — leukaemia and Hodgkin's disease are among the commonest. Leukaemia was almost a death sentence for children until the sixties. Now many children with this disease can recover, and this good news is being confirmed in a long study of child survival rates to which the Campaign is contributing in Oxford. Tumours of the kidney are another instance of striking success in survival.

To get its money the Campaign relies on 1,000 local committees dreaming up countless fund-raising ideas. It has its own trading company, and it also runs auctions of donated cars. Some of the Campaign's volunteers have eye-catching schemes, like the couple in Devon who turned a large bramble patch into a garden open to the public which brought in £3,000 over the years. There are tournaments and marathons, fun runs and markets. It's a hard slog raising money this way, but the British public give generously to cancer research.

Work After Work

The Imperial Fund has a payroll of over 800 scientists and spends more than £10 million a year. Scientists work full time at the Fund's laboratories in Lincoln's Inn Fields and Mill Hill. One recent breakthrough came from Dr John Kemshead, head of the Fund's laboratory at the Institute of Child Health. Dr Kemshead has developed a technique for removing cancer cells from bone marrow in the treatment of neuroblastoma. He recently received a cash boost from a party of city stockbrokers who ran in the London marathon for the Fund.

Another study has been undertaken by Fund scientists to identify small tumours of less than one centimetre, by attaching radioactive isotopes to tumour cells. This is expected to go into clinical trials.

At the epidemiology and clinical trials unit at Oxford university, Sir Richard Doll directs research for the Fund into diet, exposure to ionizing radiation and asbestos, and into the causes of breast cancer. One of the discoveries about this cancer is that it is more prevalent in well-off countries — with Brazil an exception where the incidence is almost up to the level of North America and Britain.

The Fund has been investigating the cancer story for decades, and its laboratory complex at Mill Hill is a leader in world research. Here scientists are studying ways in which the body's own defence system can be helped to take on and detect cancer cells when they begin to proliferate.

Both the Fund and the Campaign are proud of the fact that only 7 per cent of their income is spent on running costs, freeing 93p in every donated pound to be used directly for research. The Campaign spent £17 million in 1982 to keep its research programmes going — that was £2 million more than it actually raised in 1981. And half the £5 million it had set aside for capital expenditure was spent as well. Neither charity gets a penny from government and has to rely on imaginative fund raising, and the generosity of donors who leave money in their wills.

What is the message from the laboratory benches sponsored by these two bodies? Although discretion has been learned by scientists through a series of false starts, the signs are that the conquest of cancer will not come dramatically from one bench on one day, but that increasing numbers of minor advances will finally complete the jigsaw puzzle.

Top Ten

Royal National Lifeboat Institution

For a seafaring nation like Britain, the Royal National Lifeboat Institution is full of the salty drama which appeals to us. The British responded with overwhelming generosity to the Penlee disaster fund.

The lifeboatmen are emphatic about their voluntary status. They have opted to go out on terrifying seas to save the shipwrecked. The RNLI prefers to get its money from the public, noting realistically that this support would always be more forthcoming than government subsidy if it were nationalised.

The RNLI has been trawling coastal waters for lost seamen and women — and swimmers in difficulty — since 1824 and has saved 103,000 lives. There were 39 lifeboats then, now there are 130 large boats — from 37 to 70 feet — and 120 smaller boats, some inflatable. The first steamer went into service in 1890, petrol engines appeared in 1904 and by 1932 the fleet went diesel.

Over the past twenty-five years the RNLI report a massive increase in their seaborne rescues. Now they venture out almost 3,000 times a year from the 200 stations around our shores. Lifeboatmen save 1,000 lives every year with many hundreds more helped in medical or other emergencies. They attribute this increase to more nautical activities by the British and the popularity of sailing.

To deal with the 'leisure' casualty, the RNLI introduced the 16-foot inshore lifeboat in 1963, which has been very successful. It is quick and can work in shallow, rocky stretches. In 1972 a slightly bigger version was introduced with many sophisticated features, such as an inflatable bag which rights the boat if it is capsized. It also has a 10-mile range VHF radio and navigation lights and the engines are waterproofed by special valves designed by RNLI engineers.

After the inflatables, the fleet operates larger vessels for rescuing fishermen and other commercial crews who are in trouble further out, and equipment includes radar, intercom, echo-sounders, auto pilot and VHF radio. The biggest boat is the 70-ft *Clyde* which can remain out at sea for long periods. The last *Clyde* to be built, in 1974, cost £200,000.

A rescue operation can be a dangerous mission and in the case of

Work After Work

a shipwreck, involves helicopters from the Navy and Air Force.

Each lifeboat station is run by a voluntary committee with a secretary who will put the rescue operation in motion when the alert is given by the coastguard. Crew members are often fishermen but RNLI report that other workers are being attracted to the service. A number of auxiliary roles are attached to a station, such as shore helpers and medical advisers. There are seven divisions for the lifeboat service and paid staff include engineers and surveyors, to keep the boats in crack condition.

This first-class service costs £16 million a year to run. In order to find this, RNLI have broken the country into fourteen fund-raising districts. The districts have paid organisers and staff who direct the voluntary efforts of 2,000 branches. The volunteers stick to fairly conventional methods, like house-to-house collecting, raffles and flag days, but the cause is a popular one and a third of their income gets raised this way.

RNLI has a trading company turning out souvenirs, and a big amount comes from legacies. People also buy lifeboats. The guides and scouts, the Round Tables and the Royal British Legion have bought one each, and the young viewers of the BBC's Blue Peter programme have bought four inflatables. There is a membership scheme called Shoreline which is often taken up by sailing clubs and sea sport enthusiasts — only too aware they may need the services — but the general public also contribute to this. Members can buy insignia, but the scheme is mainly an opportunity for people to give money to the lifeboatmen.

The RNLI has an operational headquarters in Poole, Dorset, which is constantly manned. The boats are designed here in the hull and machinery drawing offices, and technical staff oversee the boats' construction at commercial yards. The depot here also manufactures many of the special parts needed.

The specialist sub-committees of the RNLI are mainly composed of volunteers, often professional people who advise on a whole range of matters from boat design to electronics, public relations, investment and construction. Firms and professional associations volunteer expertise as well.

A lot of other countries rely on volunteer lifeboat services, and when the West Germans flirted with a state-controlled service they found that the voluntary one was preferable and returned to it.

Barnardo's

Barnardo's prides itself on being an adaptable voluntary agency, adjusting to social changes. When Thomas Barnardo rescued children wandering homeless through East London streets what was required was a roof over their heads. Over a century later Barnardo's is in the forefront of preventive social work — trying to stop the break up of families. Unemployment has thrown up much social distress, particularly among the young. 'Young people face daunting problems in the 1980s and as their problems change, we are ready to change too,' said a member of staff.

In 1969 nearly half the charity's work concerned running children's homes; now that work only takes up 4 per cent of its expenditure. For Barnardo's has switched the emphasis from providing a roof for children whose families have abandoned them, to providing support for physically and emotionally handicapped children. They are now in at the deep end, caring for some very disturbed young people.

The current yearly rate of help spans 9,000 children in a variety of projects. Barnardo's works with statutory social services departments, although unhappily in some places recently ideology has come between it and a few — but only a few — Labour councils who have considered that voluntary organisations should not provide social services.

Mary Joynson, the charity's director of child care, writes in the annual report: 'The political complexion of some local authorities is affecting us more than it has done before. Some Labour-controlled councils have decided that all social services should be provided by the state, and if they cannot do so the service will not be provided. There is no room for voluntary societies in this policy. Thankfully this view is shared by only a few councils.'

A change in the population pattern, meaning fewer children in the 11–15 age group, coupled with some extensive local authority cutbacks, has caused Barnardo's to rethink its policy and to concentrate on preventive, non-residential services. The charity admits

Work After Work

this has posed an image problem because it means more work with teenagers, many of them unemployed, who have been — or are perilously close to being — in trouble with the police. Mary Joynson says that this kind of work is less appealing to the donating public than the charity's earlier work with young children. 'It is to be hoped that we can persuade people that this very difficult and very costly work is also very important,' she writes.

Barnardo's runs special homes for maladjusted, physically and mentally handicapped, hostels, day care centres, family therapy and rehabilitation centres, and community and holiday homes.

In addition, approximately 2,266 children 'at risk' are supervised in their own homes and approximately 362 in foster-homes and lodgings. Barnardo's is also a registered adoption society.

Because Barnardo's is in at the deep end it has produced some radical suggestions for finding home lives for the thousands of children in local authority care. The New Families project was a headline story because it advertised the children for adoption and fostering. In Colchester the project actually put the adverts in a shop window. This horrified a lot of people who criticised Barnardo's for selling children over the counter. But of course these were the feelings of adults and not of the children involved, who sometimes wrote up their own descriptions — making sure they indicated what sort of adoptive family they wanted — as well as being fully prepared in advance for what would happen. The hard sell certainly did not put off genuine prospective parents — they have come forward and Barnardo's reports that many new families have been found.

The New Families project operates in Scotland, East Anglia and South Wales. It tries to place physically, mentally and emotionally handicapped children of all colours, aged ten and upwards. In Scotland seventy young people have been found homes, and twenty were placed in Colchester in the first twelve months of the project there.

Barnardo's has flair. One of its more unusual experiments was a residential unit for diabetic children in Scotland to teach them how to manage their illness themselves — thereby making sure that their health did not deteriorate as they grew older.

The unit, called Cruachan, aims to educate both child and parent in the management of the disease. While the child is in residence,

Top Ten

staff at the unit include the parents and rest of the family in learning how to make diet and insulin control a part of everyday life. A badly controlled diabetic child can cause havoc within a family. The usual pattern is of frequent stays in hospital and missed school, with parents hopelessly unable to cope with the child.

Children stay at the unit for, on average, ten months, and when they go home, the unit's social worker maintains a supportive link until the family establishes a pattern of good diet control.

At Speke in Liverpool the agency is involved in an intermediate treatment project for young offenders. The children are referred from social services departments, the probation service and schools. The majority of the first groups attending the Speke centre when it opened in 1980 had committed more than one offence. Many were truants.

Speke is a mixture of voluntary and statutory co-operation: Barnardo's owns the building and pays the wages of staff running the scheme, the local authority social services department puts up a 50 per cent grant, and sends along the young 'clients'.

The treatment consists of working in groups, and the boys with criminal records who look set to continue a life of crime, are placed in long-term groups. One of the interesting features of this work is that the children are videoed during their talk sessions, a technique which is widely used in family therapy. Sport and outdoor activities are also part of the Speke programme.

So far Barnardo's is unable to claim any success for this project or whether it is having an impact on juvenile crime in the Speke area because the police collect crime statistics on a much wider, divisional basis. But Barnardo's can point to the individual success of one group containing some highly delinquent young people. This group shows little sign of re-offending by its members.

Barnardo's is also involved in training. It has a school of printing in Hertford where twenty-five apprentices are taught the most up-to-date technology including computer typesetting. The apprentices come from Barnardo's and other charities. They are disadvantaged school leavers mainly looking for a good career, and will spend four years at the school living in hostels. The school is also Barnardo's house printers, producing its promotional literature.

How does Barnardo's pay for this enormous range of services to

Work After Work

the country's children? Like most other charities it is having a lean time, and house-to-house collectors are reporting that for the first time they are getting a less than enthusiastic response from the public. Nicholas Lowe, the charity's appeals director, admits to falling short of targets in 1982, even in income from legacies.

Barnardo's 1982–3 expenditure is expected to be £31.2 million, and £3.7 million of that will be used in capital developments. There is the usual financial juggling behind the figures, with some money coming from the sale of surplus assets. Barnardo's continues to campaign, along with other charities, for VAT reform so that relief of this tax on them would enable more money to be available. So far the Chancellor has not been generous.

The biggest problem for Barnardo's is property. It needs more — to rent, buy or even borrow, promising to leave vacated premises in good condition.

Where each £1 comes from and how Barnardo's spends it
Income
Local Authority maintenance contributions 48p
Investments 7p
Legacies 22p
Voluntary contributions 23p

Expenditure
Residential and care services 80.5p
Promotion — including the salaries, pensions and expenses of appeals organisers, and printing costs 14p
Head Office administration 2.5p
Advertising, including exhibitions 1p
Cost of living increases to Barnardo's OAPs 2p

The Salvation Army

The Salvation Army is a vast empire spreading throughout the world, and like Barnardo's, is practical Christianity in action. This is a militant Christian movement with the esprit de corps of an army. Not everyone likes the uniforms and the evangelism, but the images

Top Ten

of fighting and war help its workers identify their universal enemies of hunger, poverty and despair.

This Army has 25,000 'officers' working in eighty countries, speaking 111 languages. It has 50,000 full-time employees and its schools teach 200,000 pupils. Each month the Army's famous investigation bureau locates 800 missing people. There are 150,000 in-patients and two million outpatients in its hospitals and clinics worldwide. Its hostels cope with 100,000 people nightly, and 15 million meals are served up every year.

In Britain, the Army operates a comprehensive social services network. The Sally Army's origins are part of our social history: the work with 'fallen women', the mother and baby homes, the soup runs for vagrants. The first home for women opened in 1884 in Whitechapel, after a young prostitute had been given refuge by a concerned Salvationist. During the next twenty years the Army stepped up its rescue work, providing midnight patrols, cheap food depots, prison-gate homes and hostels. The founder, William Booth, wrote *In Darkest England and the Way Out*, which mapped out the Army's social plans.

Work with families began in 1889 with a small house in Chelsea; really the forerunner of the modern maternity hospital. Homes were set up for the poor elderly, and after an advertisement for a missing person appeared in the Army paper *The War Cry*, the investigation service was set up.

Industrial homes eventually became approved schools and the Army co-operates with local authorities in the provision of some community services. The Army's social services department in Britain now runs fifty-four hostels for the homeless; forty eventide homes for the elderly; four maternity hospitals and homes; seventeen children's and teenagers' homes; eleven clubs for the forces; and thirty-five goodwill community centres.

The Army's hostels for the homeless have taken the brunt of the new social policy which is emptying psychiatric hospitals of long-stay patients. These patients are being returned to the often mythical 'community', which really means social agencies like the Salvation Army.

Rehabilitating the sub-normal and mentally handicapped from the long-stay wards is an almost impossible job in some cases, and the

Work After Work

Army admits that the more vulnerable simply become permanent residents of hostels, occupying the beds which were originally meant for those passing through who could be helped back to a more stable life.

Some hostels give a home to men who have been released from prison on bail who have nowhere to go and would otherwise have been kept in custody. The Army takes to its work with offenders with a zest to be expected from such an evangelical body. Throughout the world it visits nearly a quarter of a million prisoners and helps thousands of people discharged from prison. The Army also visits the families of prisoners, advising on financial and marital problems.

The first bail hostel was opened by the Army in Whitechapel in 1971 and magistrates often send people awaiting trial there. Courts also send young people into the care of the Salvation Army. In Oslo the staff run a rehabilitation centre to help ex-prisoners develop work skills; in Pittsburgh, USA, alcoholic offenders are given a choice by courts between gaol or a drying-out session at the Army's centre. Here they get clean pyjamas and sleep off their hangovers while preparation is made to include them in a treatment programme, which will last sixty days. Many of the alcoholics continually get to stage one of this procedure and baulk at the second, but the Army in Pittsburgh report that much of the work is successful.

Now that single mothers do find some statutory help there is less of a need for the traditional mother and baby homes, set up in the first place because of the prejudice against unmarried women. But the hostels still function as places where a young woman may stay before and after hospital delivery, and where she can have time to decide her future. In Birmingham the hostel caters for fourteen mothers and thirty-six children who have their own family rooms. Some of the mothers have jobs.

Children who have spent their whole school life in care run into problems of transition when they need to find their own homes.

In the grounds of a children's home in Liverpool teenage residents who are ready for work live in self-contained flats with minimum supervision. They discover the joys — and the irritations — of running a home, and finally they are found a place of their own away from the building.

Top Ten

The Army started a network of community centres in the 1880s which had the unpromising title of 'slum posts'. In the early days it was a fair description of the notorious inner city enclaves in the West End of London: whole families were crammed in one room, disease and poverty endemic to most of them. Although the slum posts were renamed 'goodwill centres' in 1949, a role has remained for them. These centres are now useful adjuncts to city life, offering nurseries, youth clubs, elderly clubs with service for chiropody, and advice bureaux. Holidays are organised and lunch clubs run. In Notting Hill the Army runs an emergency service for drug addicts which is used by hospitals and the police.

The Army has its own housing associations in England and Scotland, replacing the old warehouses and buildings which housed its first homeless. It is also developing a policy of varied housing — sheltered and independent flats, 'cluster' flats as well as hostels for retired people, single people and family homeless. The association's ambition is to have its own profit-generating stock to release it from government-grant reliance.

As a provider of housing, the Army registers with the government-sponsored Housing Corporation, which oversees the 3,000 housing associations in this country. In 1982–3 these associations had £556 million in England and £92 million in Scotland, made available to them to repair or build new homes. They are voluntary organisations run by committees to give cheap housing to people with no access to council housing lists.

Probably the most famous service is its missing persons bureau — 'Mrs Booth's enquiry bureau' as it was known. The investigating team is made up of nine case workers with twenty back-up staff who deal with 5,000 cases a year in Britain. They are able to call on the Army's officers worldwide in the search for someone who is reported missing.

More often than not people are reported missing years after they were last seen.

Like most detective work, a great deal of the investigation takes place by way of directories, registers and other routine sources. It can be unendurably tedious and long work. When few clues are present, the Army sometimes advertises in newspapers, apart from its own, and this does often produce results. But even success has

Work After Work

problems — not everyone found wants to be reunited, and bureau investigators have to work with tact and subtlety to bring about reconciliation.

All kinds of people go missing. Distraught husbands and wives, disgruntled teenagers. Hospitals and prisons also need help from the bureau to locate relatives of patients and prisoners.

An enormous amount of correspondence is generated by the bureau — 55,000 letters are sent out yearly from the London office, and nearly as many are received. And this costly service can sometimes draw on reserves — in a recent year the Army needed £48,000 from funds to take the bureau out of the red.

The Salvation Army likes its volunteers to be committed Christians but they do not have to be officers. Non-officer salvationists can do a variety of work, particularly in hostels, and can become 'auxiliary-Captains'. Part-time voluntary service can be given in hostels and homes for the elderly, supervising entertainment, helping elderly residents with their correspondence, taking part in occupational therapy, and so on.

The Army's biggest need is for teachers overseas, and now that a new development section has been established at the international headquarters, a number of business skills are needed for Third World countries. Just as in Britain, the skill most in demand is accountancy. Office and personnel management experience is needed to help run some of the Army's bigger institutions. Agricultural expertise — in the fields of forestry, horticulture, fish-farming and bee-keeping — is badly needed. Engineers are also in demand to help development projects.

The headquarters in London has many opportunities for managerial volunteers, and the property department needs people with surveying and architectural qualifications. Professional and business volunteers can work in the social services headquarters, the Reliance Trust Ltd, Migration and Travel Service, the Army General Insurance Corporation, the Salvationist Publishing and Supplies Ltd, and the Campfield Press.

The National Trust

Who is the third largest landowner in the United Kingdom? The

Top Ten

answer is the National Trust, a charity with housekeeping duties to the country's historical treasures, rural and architectural. This is another voluntary organisation which leapt into existence to defend Britain from the ravages of the Industrial Revolution. As the engines and mills puffed outwards from the cities in 1895, three people started a reverse movement. They were the housing reformer Octavia Hill, solicitor Sir Robert Hunter who had a particular fear for rural Surrey, and a parson from the Lake District, Canon Hardwicke Rawnsley.

The Trust was formed as a non-profitmaking trading company able to buy land for the country so that it could be preserved. Its first land purchase was clifftops at Barmouth Estuary in North Wales; the first building was a clergyman's house in Sussex. Several years later the Trust took a step to ensure the inviolability of its property, incorporated by an Act of Parliament which gave it a mandate to preserve national history. This prevented the property from being sold without the permission of Parliament. So the National Trust's capital assets cannot be sold off to raise money, when times are hard.

A later threat to the buying up of the great country houses was death duties and tax. Another Act of Parliament, in 1937, enabled the Trust to hold houses and their contents. The Trust's Country House Scheme was inspired by the gift of Blickling Hall, Norfolk, from the Marquess of Lothian. The scheme has probably been a lifeline for many of our nobility, as well as for the Trust. Under it they can hand over their estate and its contents, with an endowment fund for maintenance, and they and their descendants continue to live there rent-free while part of the house is open to the public.

In this way many properties of outstanding historical interest can continue as homes, rather than as museums. Knole in Kent, Powys Castle and Nostell Priory in West Yorkshire still house the original families or their descendants. Smaller houses which were the homes of writers, poets, statesmen and entertainers have also been bought — Bernard Shaw and Beatrix Potter among them.

The British have a great affection for the National Trust. Nearly seven million people a year visit the houses and gardens — Sissinghurst among them — abbeys, windmills, lakes, bird sanctuaries and ancient monuments.

Work After Work

The Trust owns 450,000 acres, and in 1965 it launched Enterprise Neptune to capture parts of our coastline so that it would be protected from development. Neptune raised £2 million in 1973 and now there are 400 protected miles around our shores.

The outgoings of the National Trust are probably amongst the biggest in the voluntary field. Conservation is a costly business, from the restoration of canvases to the upkeep of crumbling ancient masonry: and the bill runs to £25 million a year. The gardens alone cost £2 million a year to maintain. The Trust meets these costs partly with membership fees from more than a million people. Even so, it has money worries, and relies on legacies and gifts.

For the amount of work to be done, the Trust has a small full-time executive staff of 170 covering the London headquarters and the seven regions. But the Trust's executive committee, appointed by its Council, mounts a large voluntary effort throughout the country, calling on the freely given services of professional men and women in the fields of architecture, fine arts, forestry, horticulture, estate management, public relations and conservation of all kinds.

A lot of people apply to the Trust for paid work but vacancies do not often occur. However, expertise in the many areas of conservation is in demand. Here is a rundown of the occupations needed by the Trust.

For example, land agents, who manage properties and estates including buildings of historic interest, are much in demand. Agents are usually chartered surveyors. Conservation advisory staff are needed too: forestry and horticulturist specialists, stationed in Cirencester, advising on rural management. Also in short supply are gardeners, woodlands staff and wardens: gardeners need to be able to manage the garden as well as have practical experience; whereas woodland staff plant, weed, fence and carry out clearance work. Forest management comes into the higher grade of regional forester; wardens have to have tact in dealing with the public, and they have to supervise other outdoor workers.

Historical building representatives are also essential to the Trust; they arrange houses with their contents for public display. And so are architects: property is usually in the care of a professional practising in the immediate area. Restoration, however, is often on a freelance basis. But in textile conservation, voluntary workers at

Top Ten

workrooms in Knole, Blickling and Hughenden, offer their services. Archaeology too is a relevant discipline: the Trust's possessions are being documented and the help of voluntary advisers is sought regionally. As are administrators: they run the larger houses, organising maintenance and security. These are usually higher grade executives aged between forty and fifty-five who know how to handle the public and create a good atmosphere at the stately home.

Publicity is a large part of the Trust's work and, regionally, information officers are involved in lecturing, recruitment, advertising, organising exhibitions and fund raising. People with a journalistic or public relations background are ideal for this type of work.

Accounting financially is a major job for the Trust and a specialist team is employed at Melksham, Wiltshire, where the Trust's computer is based. As with any charity, wizards with figures are always needed.

Catering opportunities are increasing as the Trust opens more shops and restaurants — open only, of course, in the summer. The management is handled by a director of trading, a buyer and catering adviser. The Trust says it wants more trained catering staff.

Legally, the Trust is served by four full-time solicitors, although recruiting for this service is allegedly difficult.

Secretaries are often required by the Trust, regionally and in London, and because they work from small offices they learn a lot about the work of the organisation.

Recently, the Trust has been aware that the continuation of its work in preserving the national heritage will depend on future generations, so it has begun to develop a policy of involving young people. A small group stationed at Cliveden, Buckinghamshire, direct the youth campaign, and an education adviser has been appointed.

Acorn Camps are popular with young outdoor enthusiasts who like to take part in conservation programmes. Staying in simple accommodation, they spend a week in a location which needs forestry clearance, wall or hedge maintenance, landscaping or creating coastal paths for the public. Young people are also encouraged to join voluntary groups in their own towns to keep their own rural backyards properly preserved.

Work After Work

Save the Children Fund

This charity has a very committed president who hops abroad to see how the fieldworkers are managing, and she gets cross with photographers who catch her out on these trips. Princess Anne likes to see for herself the conditions under which children in the developing world try to live. She has given much publicity to the Fund which has undoubtedly helped it into its position as Britain's largest international children's charity.

There are some unpalatable facts about poor countries which can seem unreal to a country where most people eat daily. Save the Children points out that 20 per cent of children born in the developing world die before their first birthday; that those who don't will face life malnourished; and less than half will go to school.

The Fund began its international work in 1919 and decided in 1926 that it should help out at home too. In Britain the Fund looks after 10,000 children daily, with 75 per cent government money towards the yearly UK budget of £4 million.

The bulk of the work abroad concerns health, nutrition, education and vocational training. The fund is active in 57 countries, helping half a million children. One of its most important current programmes is the STOP polio campaign, which ambitiously aims to wipe out the disease for the world's children by the end of the century. Pilot campaigns in Malawi, Swaziland and Lesotho in 1980 were successful. The Fund worked with the countries' governments and the World Health Organisation to maintain the immunisation programme, and supplied equipment to keep polio vaccine at the correct temperature — vital to preserve its effectiveness.

Another killer is diarrhoeal disease and one of the reasons is that a traditional remedy in many places is to stop a child drinking, which merely accelerates dehydration. The Fund is joining forces with other organisations in Zimbabwe to encourage mothers to give suffering children doses of oral rehydration solution — simply salt and sugar in water.

Many charities working against overwhelming poverty soon discover that the big development programmes often miss the point, that much simpler schemes can change the picture dramatically for deprived peoples. The Fund describes the world's 'poverty belt' as

Top Ten

existing between the Tropics of Cancer and Capricorn, and it concentrates its efforts there, with workers teaching villagers how to overcome some of their disadvantages.

Health problems are largely due to poor sanitation, a lesson which the West learned itself not so very long ago. Save the Children teams often include engineers to set up clean water projects and pass on the techniques to locals. The Fund is beginning to see a pattern in its work — first going into a country stricken with famine or other disaster to deliver emergency services, and then staying around to help rural populations build a better life.

An example of successful 'passed on' expertise is the story of Boroma in North West Somalia, where a refugee shanty camp near the town has now developed into a village. Refugees learned from Save the Children teams how to fix up water supplies, organise primary schools and arrange food deliveries. Even in the town of Boroma the Fund has helped the local population improve its own services, including laying on water and electricity for the hospital.

The Fund commits itself to staying in a region until it can pass its projects over to the government to continue. In Nepal Princess Anne witnessed the signing of an agreement between the government and the Fund for projects in the country covering health and hygiene education. In the Nepalese clinics there will be formal training sessions for local medical students and nurses.

Wherever possible the Fund keeps its own visiting teams to a minimum and employs local staff. In certain projects, like Jamalpur in Bangladesh, there are no expatriates. The training scheme for health workers there has had a gratifying result: in five years the neonatal death rate has been cut by half. Governments often seek the help of the Fund in their own nutrition programmes, as in Papua New Guinea where it is supplying an adviser to the Ministry of Health. Its nutritionists are also advising in refugee camps in Ethiopia. In Honduras the SCF teams have even imported the very British allotment, calling them village vegetable gardens.

Training has become a cornerstone of the Save the Children Fund's policy. Recent programmes have dealt exclusively with projects to train primary health care teams. In Binga, Zimbabwe, the fund is paying for eight-week courses for locally selected trainees. By this simple training it is hoped that 80,000 people in the outlying

Work After Work

areas will have some access to medical care over the next five years, as well as help with nutrition, sanitation and preventive medicine such as immunisation.

In Britain the problems may be different, but there are still problems of underprivilege. Save the Children has been something of a pioneer at home too, in finding new ways of caring for the young. It helps children in hospital, in gypsy camps, refugee children settling in the United Kingdom, and young people caught up in cycles of deliquency. Mobile playgroups visit gypsy camps to help acclimatise pre-school children; there are thirteen centres in the United Kingdom for refugees such as the Boat People; and in Northern Ireland the Fund spends £$\frac{1}{4}$ million on projects for children. In hospitals trained Fund staff can dissolve some of the fear and tension young patients feel.

Like Barnardo's, Save the Children has become interested in intermediate treatment for young offenders. They are in the forefront of this new form of handling the young criminal, or the child at risk of becoming one. Five intermediate centres take in the delinquents and work with them and their families. The Fund also has a small number of residential schools and centres for emotionally disturbed children who can't attend ordinary school.

Throughout the world Save the Children spends £36,000 *a day*. The recession affected its income in 1981–2 when gifts dropped, and the total income fell to £13.2 million. Some projects were rescheduled for later, but the Fund says its long-term projects are not jeopardised. Its bill for staff in the United Kingdom (766 people) was £4.2 million during 1981–2. More than 1,000 people were employed on the overseas programme. Over the years the Save the Children Fund has raised and spent over £100 million, and it claims that 85p in every £1 goes directly to relief and welfare work.

In raising its money Save the Children has made a direct appeal to the business world, offering valuable spinoffs to companies who became involved in joint fund-raising schemes. Firms which take part in commercial promotions benefit through publicity, customer support and increased sales, and the scheme has gone down well.

At Christmas '82 the International Stores chain gave customers spending more than £10 a pack of the charity's cards, donating 5p for every one to the Fund; £200,000 was raised through a label-collecting promotion at Fine Fare stores; £25,000 came from an Express Dairy 'drink more pintas' campaign.

The Red Cross

The Red Cross is one of those charities in at the sharp end. Worldwide, there is on average an SOS for help in natural or man-made disasters every three weeks.

Three organisations make up the international picture: the International Committee of the Red Cross (ICRC); the League of Red Cross Societies; and the scores of Red Cross Societies based in most countries organising their own national programmes, sending people and supplies overseas when asked.

The ICRC is a sensitive organisation working with the backing of international law. Delegates, who visit scenes of battles anywhere in the world, are Swiss nationals, and as such have an ingrained neutrality. This is imperative in conflict when the merest suspicion of sympathy for one side might halt a relief programme for injured and starving soldiers and civilians. Although the ICRC has the four Geneva Conventions behind it, there sometimes have to be lengthy negotiations with army commanders before Red Cross shipments of personnel and supplies get a safe guarantee. Even then it doesn't always work — as in the case of three Red Cross workers killed in a Rhodesia/Zimbabwe mission.

The League exists to coordinate international help from its member nations during emergency relief operations. It also helps countries start their own societies, and encourages disaster-prone countries like those in earthquake or hurricane zones, to organise early warning systems and relief preparation.

The British Red Cross Society is a paramedic organisation which devotes a lot of its time to training the public in simple first aid and nursing skills. Most of this work is given freely, and the BRCS estimated that in 1981 its volunteers donated £27 million worth of semi-skilled work, based on average rates of pay. Out of an income of £11 million in that year, £9 million was spent in Britain on the Society's work, and £2 million went overseas, helping out in those three-weekly disaster appeals. The Society sometimes feels that it

Work After Work

doesn't give as much to these as it would like, but unfortunately the money has to come out of its general fund. Because a lot of tragic events do not get reported, they do not stir a generous national response. 'Small' disasters like earthquakes in distant countries don't get wide media coverage, but it's unfair to blame newspapers and television for this as they are already criticised for carrying too much bad news.

The BRCS runs certified first aid courses for the public given under the instruction of doctors, nurses and social workers and helped by trained Red Cross instructors. These courses range over the new Health and Safety regulations which appoint named employees to be in charge of medical kits at work, emergency preparations, accident coverage and family nursing designed to help people coping with disabled or sick relatives.

Sometimes personnel from home go to British outposts to help with training programmes, like visiting the Belize Red Cross which needed to put together a post-hurricane relief organisation.

As representatives of a paramedical body, volunteers use their training covering major public gatherings like sports events, and offering services to GPs' group practices and health centres. The Red Cross visits housebound patients under the supervision of the practice nurse.

The Society also runs a transport and escort service which will take disabled or frail elderly people on business or pleasure trips. The service runs more than 3,000 trips a year, from cars to Red Cross ambulances and undertakes to see the passenger safely from door to door, with wheelchair. If arrangements have to be made for the wheelchair to be transported by train on another stage of the journey, the escort will handle that. 'We don't just dump people at their destinations,' says the service organiser. Because of the cost of petrol the BRCS charges for this service, but the amount is kept to the minimum necessary to cover fuel.

The BRCS are good all-round friends to disabled people. They organise holidays — and arrange the necessary transport. They have holiday homes for the handicapped, homes for pre-convalescent patients, retirement homes, and a number of other hostels. BRCS Branches have applied to REACH for Appeals Officers and Organisers of Branch centres.

Top Ten

A service not generally known is the tracing bureau, which finds lost relatives over continents, and has had success linking up families who have been split up since the Second World War. The BRCS card index contains 16,000 entries in the Indo-Chinese section and 152,000 in the general section.

The bureau traces an average of twenty-eight people a month. In some years well over 1,000 of the tracings have been families separated by the last world war, like the case of Mr Josef Samek who was arrested by Russian soldiers forty-one years ago and was recently traced to Warsaw by the Red Cross and reunited with his daughter who lives in England.

British volunteers do see overseas service. They are seconded to branches in other countries where there has been an emergency. This can be from Ethiopia to the South Pacific. Africa seems to be the place most torn by war and natural disaster. Africans have faced starvation and drought in Angola, Kenya, Mozambique, Karamoja. Some medical teams are confronted with the aftermath of massacres and have to mount emergency operations with the minimum of equipment.

Before the 1850s casualties of war usually died where they were on the battlefield. But the battle of Solferino changed that. By chance a Swiss businessman, Henry Dunant, was visiting the region of the fighting and saw the appalling scenes of suffering. Dying soldiers clawed their way to villages, and Dunant, forgetting what he had gone to the region for, threw himself into rescue work. Although the villagers were not keen to assist him, he persuaded them to take part in salvaging some of the human wrecks.

After this Dunant wrote down his experience in a book. Later he was joined by four other Swiss businessmen and they began the Committee of Five. This blossomed into an international committee and in 1864 the first Geneva Convention for the Amelioration of the Wounded of Armies in the Field was signed.

The first soldiers to benefit were those fighting the Franco-Prussian war in 1870. Unfortunately most of the Red Cross work was to bury the dead. But one of the significant events was that Red Cross Societies — including the British — sent relief to both sides. The whole movement was kept working from then on, and a massive effort was organised during the First World War when volunteers

Work After Work

looked after the wounded, drove trains and ambulances, set up hospitals and organised convalescent homes in Britain for survivors.

The International Committee also visits political prisoners — more than 300,000 during the past thirty-five years. A man in a Latin American jail told a Red Cross visitor: 'The guards threaten to kill us every day. But as long as you come to visit us, they wouldn't dare.'

Help the Aged

For the retired — or about to be — Help the Aged may be a bit too near home. Will we need them when we hit the seventy mark? And is a picture of British elderly freezing and starving an accurate one?

People mainly blunder into old age. There is no real psychological preparation for it and it is quite likely that what we were as young and middle-aged people, we'll continue to be in our old age, except frailer. If we have not been community-spirited during our working lives, there is little likelihood that we will develop an interest in community events later. In other words, personality does play a big part in what happens to us in old age.

A problem which is being increasingly recognised, at least by doctors, is the physical damage caused to the elderly by insidious hypothermia. The temperature does not have to be below zero for people to fall victim to this condition — toddlers sitting on the side of swimming baths with their teeth chattering can get it. So can an elderly person sitting at home alone; wary of high heating bills he or she may well cheat on the heat and fall victim as a result.

Hypothermia was put on the medical map by the late Dr Geoffrey Taylor. Until then the popular image was of mountaineers and explorers dying from exposure. But it is more and more probable that a lot of elderly confusion can be accounted for by a lack of body heat. Agencies like Help the Aged have tried to tackle this by information campaigns directed to the old themselves, and by pressure on government for higher pensions. Help the Aged says that 700,000 people face the hazard of hypothermia every winter because their homes are just not warm enough. Once body temperature has gone below 32°C (90°F) consciousness is impaired, blood pressure falls and the condition may progress to heart block. At this stage, hospital treatment is necessary.

Help the Aged is not just for the elderly poor — although poverty is the biggest problem for many pensioners. Loneliness affects all classes and may often trigger earlier senility. A psychogeriatrician writing in a doctor's journal described two circumstances of the elderly: ' "Happily married with surviving children living nearby": almost any devastation can be borne. "Grumpy, self-opinionated divorcee with children scattered around the globe": and much less in the way of illness or disability may equate with breakdown and the release of painful, insatiable symptoms.'

To combat loneliness Help the Aged has tried new tactics. It has advocated day centres, which have got away from the dreaded image of the 'old people's club'. Day centres have a lot more going for them, particularly services which elderly people might not find elsewhere, like chiropody. The agency gives grants to get the centres started, and has run many appeals to buy a fleet of minibuses to take members to centres. For the two million old people living alone in this country, such social gatherings could make a major difference in their lives.

An obstacle to enjoyable retirement is the spectre of disablement after illness. Help the Aged has initiated projects for rehabilitation since 1975, working in cooperation with statutory services. For example, a unit at Ipswich hospital is treating 2,000 stroke victims a year, who started their treatment at the general hospital and then moved to the rehabilitation unit. The agency is supporting two other units, in Richmond and Brent. In the Brent health district, which covers 31,000 retired people, there was no prospect of government money for a unit, so Help the Aged got moving with an appeal and the £300,000 day hospital adjacent to the Central Middlesex hospital was built.

REACH has supplied this charity with volunteers experienced in financial and committee work.

The inspiration for Help the Aged was not elderly men and women in Britain, but old people abroad, victims of disasters and famines. The group of businessmen who started the organisation sent supplies to Skopje after the earthquake, to Nigerian refugees and to the Vietnamese. But in 1966 a research project into slum

Work After Work

housing in Britain showed them squalor and despair much nearer home. There were 350,000 old people living in slum conditions. Even today, there are $1\frac{1}{2}$ million elderly living in houses without inside lavatories.

Help the Aged began housing associations, dedicated to providing sheltered housing, and their Anchor Housing Association now carries out a lot of purpose-built work throughout the country. In the seventies the agency tried to alert the rest of the community to its elderly, especially those living alone. The Good Neighbour Charter provided good news copy for local newspapers reminding readers to keep an eye open for old people in their street who failed to take in the milk or who were not seen for days at a time. The campaign urged people to do some shopping for their elderly neighbours, especially in winter.

At the same time Help the Aged improved communication to old people themselves, reminding nearly a million people that they were not receiving supplementary benefits to which they were entitled.

In Britain we are moving towards a population which will be predominantly elderly. In 1931 there were ten middle-aged people for each person over the age of seventy-five. In 1991 that ratio will be down to three-to-one. By the year 2000 the over-seventy-fives in the population will have increased by one-fifth from today's level and the over-eighty-fives by a half. At present 40 per cent of all acute NHS beds are occupied by the elderly, so in medical circles at least, there is real panic at the coming 'geriatric explosion'.

But they are the 'bad news' statistics. There are figures to support a more positive approach, like the fact that 80 per cent of the over-eighties do not suffer from age-related dementia. What alarms people is the prospect of so many old people — helped to their long years by the better nutrition and sanitation of this century — becoming mentally infirm and unable to manage their lives. But few succumb to pathological dementia and much of the vulnerability of the elderly is caused by depressing loneliness and social neglect.

It is for groups like Help the Aged, and Age Concern, to work on the conscience of the nation in the next decades before the 'explosion' hits us. Large-scale social problems could be averted if the 'young' elderly entered the last phase of their lives as alert, interested, social beings. Often years of neglect means that by the

Top Ten

time a doctor is called in to an ageing relative, a local authority home is the only option. The neglect can cause a vicious circle. The old person may be grumpy, self-obsessed and selfish, which in turn puts off many family members from visiting or inviting. This, of course, merely confirms to the lonely old person the extent of his or her neglect.

Long-stay geriatric wards are rightly despised. They really are dumping grounds and a sign of failure. Some old people's homes are not much better and these options are last resorts that could be avoided if more was done earlier in people's lives to equip them socially for old age. In some ways Help the Aged's most important role is as a campaigning body, although the day centres, and rehabilitation units play a big part. The agency has gone from a budget of £111,765 in 1963 to over £7 million twenty years later. It will need much more money and help in the next twenty.

HARRY LYTHGOE

Age 70
Previous occupation Consultant engineer and power station manager.
Occupation now President of the Bolton Mountain Rescue Team.

The rescue team is an entirely voluntary effort, so the forty young members, who are aged between twenty and thirty, pay their own expenses on training weekends and call-outs. They are alerted to missing walkers on the North Pennine moors and hills by the police and go out an average of six times a year. Unlike the Lake District and Welsh mountains, Pennine walkers are less likely to notify people of their walking plans and there is often a tragic delay of up to two days before neighbours alert police. 'We know that we are often searching for people already dead', says the rescue team leader Bob Hutchinson.

The team is also engaged in training programmes aimed at teaching young people how to avoid hill accidents. Members help in mountaincraft classes via the Duke of Edinburgh

Work After Work

Award Scheme. The team already spends a lot of time training and organising rescue work, so the job of raising funds has given them a headache. A solution has been to organise one big sponsored Pennine walk a year to be split with local charities, 'then we can forget money raising for a year', says Mr Hutchinson. It was at this point in 1982 that Mr Lythgoe put in an appearance:

'I organised the 15-mile walk for 1,000 people and we raised £4,000, and half that went to my team. I had to negotiate with sponsors and with all the landowners over whose ground the walk took place. After that the team asked me to be their president and I happily accepted. They've asked me to take on another year — and another walk — and I've agreed. What pleases me so much is to see young people so full of enthusiasm, giving a great deal of time, effort and their own money to this kind of work. They pay for their own exercises and practices.

'I've never been a walker myself and I think it's a bit late to start now but my main function is supporting the team and helping to attract money for its work. I have a lot of local contacts which I can put to good use. The team uses Landrovers but can't possibly afford new ones.

'So I am negotiating with the Chief Constable of Manchester Police to buy one of their old vehicles, at the right sort of price.

'People say "The Bolton Mountain Rescue Team? — but there aren't any mountains in Bolton!" What they don't realise is that we rescue a lot of people who are just out walking on the moors and get lost. I have enjoyed this retirement job and I wouldn't mind taking on more work for charity. I wouldn't like to think of all this experience going to waste, and I don't want money from it.'

Bob Hutchinson comments: 'He's invaluable to us. He is highly qualified and with a degree in mechanical engineering he helps us with our vehicle maintenance. He has a lot of influential friends who can help us with necessary supplies and he can spend time negotiating with police and local authorities which saves us having to take time off work.'

Top Ten

Harry Lythgoe (left) Bolton Mountain Rescue Team president, up on the moor in front of the team's truck with map of sponsored walk route and other team members Carole Eaves (centre) and Klare Twist (right.)

Useful addresses
Oxfam 274 Banbury Road, Oxford. Tel. 0865-56777
Cancer Research Campaign 2 Carlton House Terrace, London SW1. Tel. 01-581 3678.
Imperial Cancer Research Fund PO Box No. 123, Lincoln's Inn Fields, London WC2. Tel. 01-242 0200.
Royal National Lifeboat Institution West Quay Road, Poole, Dorset. Tel. Poole 6711 33.
The Salvation Army 101 Queen Victoria Street, London EC4. Tel. 01-236 5222.
The National Trust 42 Queen Anne's Gate, London SW1. Tel. 01-222 9251.
Save The Children Fund Mary Datchelor House, 17 Grove Lane, London SE5. Tel. 01-703 5400.
British Red Cross Society 9 Grosvenor Crescent, London SW1. Tel. 01-235 5454.

Work After Work

Help The Aged 32 Dover Street, London W1. Tel. 01-499 0972.
Barnardo's Tanners Lane, Barkingside, Ilford, Essex. Tel. 01-550 8822.

Reference work
North-South: A Programme for Survival. The Brandt Report. Pan World Affairs. £1.95.

CHAPTER SEVEN

ON A JET PLANE

If you like the philosophy of 'working after work' in the white economy, why not be really bold and give some practical help to the developing world by taking your expertise to them?

Put on a safari suit, get inoculated, take your wife or husband, and fly out to somewhere exotic like Barbados to help the local community expand its retail trading, develop its environmental safety, plan its training needs or open a brewery. And it won't cost you a penny.

Retired British executives are doing this in fifty-four different countries. They go as guests of the company or government in the host country and their trips are organised by a charity called British Executive Service Overseas (BESO). This is a thirteen-year-old group financed by industry, commerce and the government through the Overseas Development Administration. BESO deals in experience: it needs technologists, management specialists skilled in systems, methods and supervision, and professional managers from nearly all fields.

Executives go abroad on specific assignments for terms ranging from a couple of weeks to six months. They can be retired, or about to retire, or in some cases mid-career secondments can be arranged to help a manager develop his or her career. BESO makes and pays the travel arrangements, including the inoculations, pays a clothing allowance and picks up the bill for travelling expenses in the United Kingdom before the trip. Once in the host country, accommodation and subsistence is provided by the government or company who made the request for help.

One bonus with this scheme is that spouses — or boyfriends or girlfriends — can go along too, guests of BESO. As retirement is

Work After Work

supposed to be when you start seeing more of your partner, this is an ideal arrangement.

BESO, itself run by retired executives, pays some care and attention to arranging the trips. Politically unstable countries are given a wide berth; no one wants to end up being interrogated at airports when they are on a voluntary stint. And accommodation has to be right. BESO has international representatives who negotiate the projects and brief the volunteer, and they also check that the accommodation will be of a certain standard.

There is, of course, a lot of what is called enlightened self-interest in all this.

This form of aid to poor countries does not come without strings attached, but the British business community says that by helping them we help ourselves. By giving expertise — which would cost upwards of £300 a day and first-class travel expenses on the open market — to a new manufacturer in a developing country, they will progress sufficiently to want to buy our goods. Put this way, the third world could be helping to diminish unemployment here. BESO says that 50,000 British jobs are kept going by the £300 million exports a year which flow from our overseas aid programme.

About 160 countries and dependencies make up the 'third world', and 73 per cent of the world's population lives in them. More than 55 per cent of working age people in them are unemployed or underemployed; and 80 per cent of the world's children live there. A quarter of a million of those children suffer the blindness of malnutrition. The average weekly income of an Ethiopian worker is £1.

With facts like these staring us in the face the Brandt report becomes the only real workable policy for the world's future. The poor southern countries need massive help from the northern countries, and whereas organisations like BESO are small-scale, and admittedly aid is a two-way deal, it is a first step in the right direction.

In its manufacturing industries, developing countries mostly lack middle management skills. A retired textile technologist who did four BESO assignments in two years says that although the industries were varied, from cotton spinning to woollen weaving, the big problem was always the same: lack of experienced management.

BESO copes with an average of 130 assignments a year but says

On a Jet Plane

that its requests for personnel far exceed this. More than 1,000 executives are on the register. BESO volunteers handle projects in both private and public sector. A printing consultant made a twelve-day fact-finding trip to Jordan when the Ministry of Education wanted to start a printing company to produce educational books; his report covered management, marketing and equipment buying, suggesting a capital outlay of £540,000, and most of the purchases could be made in the UK.

A town planner spent a month in Syria producing technical reports for the construction of a sewage works and factories; in the Philippines, a retired NCB electrical engineer has helped plan major investment in the private coal industry.

A former personnel manager from the United Africa Company helped work out the personnel needs of a 721-bed hospital in Karachi; a former packaging manager went to Cyprus to help a struggling toiletry manufacturer. They've asked him back three times.

Assignments are diverse, from assisting population censuses in the Cayman Islands to banking and crop drying in Fiji. Volunteers report high job satisfaction. So far, BESO have not sent many women abroad, mainly because the generation which began to develop careers in business and professions has not yet reached retirement age. One businesswoman who carried out a fascinating study in Thailand was Mrs Doris Young who ran her own furniture company from 1943 until recently. Mrs Young is an expert on timber — she has travelled widely buying it for furniture and she is experienced in furniture design and manufacture. BESO sent Mrs Young to Thailand to help a company which had acquired felling rights in forests. The Thai government has a replanting scheme which requires old rubber plantations to be felled. Was this wood any use in furniture manufacturing? the company wanted to know. Mrs Young spent a fortnight looking at the rubber trees. They were as hard as teak and she thought they were as suitable as beech for furniture. But the Thais had got the price wrong for an overseas market. She recommended pre-fabrication of furniture from the wood, to be assembled in the overseas market, which would make it competitive. Her advice is being taken by the company which is going ahead to buy a pilot plant to make up the components. And

Work After Work

she is using her marketing knowledge of Britain to help the company find customers.

'I didn't know a word of the language,' she says, 'but they gave me an interpreter and a chauffeur. The Thais have found a synthetic substitute for rubber which is more durable for car tyres, but now they are left with 95,000 acres of rubber trees. This wood has its limitations. The trees grow too high and are not stable. I suggested they buy plant and make partly assembled school and garden furniture, and I'd be happy to go back and help them set up the machines.'

Mrs Young's furniture company is now run by her daughter — the second generation of women to steer the family business which was started by Mrs Young's grandfather. She is now in semi-retirement and available as a consultant to her daughter.

'I would like to go on some more BESO trips,' she says. 'I am a keen horticulturalist and would consider advising in this field. I think sending out advice to developing countries is a better way than giving money, which can go adrift. Responsibility does not end with giving money, and they do need our help. I was in the West Indies recently and saw imported orange squash being sold at £1.20 a bottle when oranges were growing everywhere.'

Voluntary Service Overseas

You may think that Voluntary Service Overseas (VSO) is just for the young. It certainly has a reputation for committed young volunteers giving up their jobs in the United Kingdom and throwing themselves into development schemes in poor countries. But VSO report a regularly increasing number of older people applying to them for work overseas. Although there is a theoretical ceiling of sixty-five, VSO recruitment officers say that there is positive discrimination in favour of the mature volunteer, maturity and experience often counting just as much, if not more, than qualifications.

One recent recruitment was a fifty-nine-year-old social worker who is spending two years in a Sri Lankan community development programme. 'He's working in a slum,' admits Brian Passman,

On a Jet Plane

business and social officer for VSO. He originally left his job in order to gain a higher qualification so that he could lecture — but then, because of the government's education squeeze, finished up as an insurance salesman.

'We wanted someone for this project who had a wide variety of community based skills,' says Mr Passman. 'Social work experience on its own would not have been enough, but he had built his own home extension and had experience of building, rewiring and plumbing — making him an ideal candidate for the job.'

VSO volunteers are paid a salary equivalent to a local wage — enough to live on but not enough to maintain commitments back home, which makes it a possibility for a retired person whose children and mortgage are offloaded. Married couples can go overseas but the spouse has to volunteer too. A typical older applicant would be a businessman who sells up on retirement, puts between £20,000 and £30,000 in the bank and then goes abroad with his wife for some voluntary work. Volunteers are paid three grants to cover their service, which is usually longer than BESO trips. The first covers clothes and equipment in the host country, the mid-term grant pays for a short holiday, and the third re-equips the volunteer for coming home.

What skills are needed? VSO has five development desks: business and social; technical; education (VSO reports many more older teachers volunteering); health; and agriculture.

The VSO programme on agriculture aims to help individual farmers achieve self-reliance. Projects use subsistence farmers, unemployed youths, women's groups and refugees and training is an integral part. VSO workers stay at the drawing board too — managing, planning, evaluating and researching. All this stays at the level which is practical for the small farmer.

In the technical arena finding a way to cleanse polluted water has proved one of the major ambitions. Technical volunteers are involved both in training in the use of effective machinery and in operating it on specific projects like road building and improved water supplies. Engineers solve problems with whatever skills and cheap materials are on hand.

Developing countries are moving towards full primary education so the next need is for secondary education. In addition to science

Work After Work

and language many VSO teachers are training in vocational subjects like home economics and commerce.

VSO health workers can find themselves involved in public sanitation measures, like improving water supplies and sewage disposal, which can be central to better health. But the VSO health desk can never get enough volunteers because developing countries are confronted with enormous health problems based on malnutrition and poor sanitation.

Business volunteers are helping to set up small businesses and co-operatives, and are teaching commercial skills. Social workers sent overseas do not use their formal training as this is mostly inappropriate to the countries' needs, but they are helping with community projects which are informally organised, and which require flexibility in the volunteer.

MRS STELLA WENTWORTH-SHEILDS

Age 65
Previous occupation Advertising sales executive.
Occupation now Promotional work with the Intermediate Technology Development Group in London, set up in 1965 by Dr Ernst Schumacher of Small is Beautiful fame.

ITDG concentrates on helping areas in need, socially, economically and technically. Technology suitable for the particular circumstances is suggested, because ITDG is interested in spreading knowledge rather than aid. It is funded by the Overseas Development Administration to the tune of £350,000 a year as well as from trusts, companies and governments. The group has carried out commissioned work on behalf of the World Bank and for agencies like Christian Aid and Oxfam. In many cases sophisticated technology is not appropriate for an area because of the high cost and difficulty of sustaining it.

Mrs Wentworth-Sheilds has been helping the ITDG fund-raising effort, particularly in the promotion of the 1983

On a Jet Plane

sponsored marathon run across the 2,500-mile length of the Himalayas by two brothers, Richard and Adrian Crane. She says of this project:

'We have been promoting the run to radio, television, newspapers and companies and to individuals interested in athletics as well as the East. We've consulted *Who's Who* for the names, and we've been looking for ex-diplomats and army people. It's surprising how much time it takes. I originally said I'd do half a day a week but I've been going in four times a week; you really get involved and they are such nice people.

'I enjoy working at this level but I don't want any major responsibility at my age. My life has been on magazines selling advertising and it has been a very full and tiring life. When I retired at sixty-two I didn't want anyone to rely on me for anything any more! I'd had a husband and clients relying on me, people being disappointed if I couldn't meet arrangements so by this time I was workshy. I didn't want any more commitments. I enjoyed going along to classes at the City Literary Institute and no-one was upset if I didn't go.

'But my nephew badgered me about doing some voluntary work as he said I'd moulder and I still had a residue. However, the first 'job' I went for was selling subscriptions for a community magazine to help them make up for the loss of a £60,000 government grant. That horrified me. That was getting on the treadmill again. I said No!'

Useful addresses
BESO Institute of Directors, 116–119 Pall Mall, London SW1. Tel. 01-839 1233.
VSO 9 Belgrave Square, London SW1. Tel. 01-235 5191.

Work After Work

Mrs. Wentworth-Sheilds helped put these runners into the news pages of British papers. Adrian Crane (left) and his brother Richard tackling the Himalayas on their marathon sponsored run.

CHAPTER EIGHT

IN THE COMMUNITY

In the country

If rural England is where you've set your heart when you retire, don't assume you will be too far from any action to be useful to a voluntary group. There's nothing to stop you starting one of your own.

Although the recession has undoubtedly persuaded many people that they are more or less impotent in the face of national and international economic changes, they have begun to wonder whether or not they can influence what goes on in their own locality, rural or urban. This trend is amply illustrated by the increasing number of jobs advertised in national papers for a whole range of local development agencies, co-operative development agencies, systems for sponsoring and supporting new small enterprises.

Many local authorities have begun to redefine their own roles. No longer fully satisfied with trying to tempt firms to their areas with infrastructures, factories, rates holidays and the rest, they are increasingly going into the money lending business, funding advice and feasibility studies and reviewing their purchasing policies. Often for the first time they are seeking to open up relationships with local business and unions, and with local voluntary organisations.

Much of this activity is focused on the areas of highest unemployment and the localities where the decimation of industry has been the most noticeable. The most urgent priority has been given to the inner cities and the old industrial areas in Northern Ireland, Scotland, Wales and the North of England. A good example of this is the combined Department of the Environment and business initiative to try to regenerate parts of Liverpool in the wake of the riots.

Work After Work

There is plenty of evidence that the approach is catching on and an increasing number of initiatives are sprouting in rural areas. Country areas have not only been hard hit by recession; they have missed out on some government help like the Youth Opportunities Programme and now the Youth Training Scheme because these schemes have been designed with urban circumstances in mind. In many ways these schemes discriminate against potential beneficiaries in the countryside simply because their rules are insensitively applied to rural problems.

The issue of how rural areas can emerge with a decent level of economic activity apart from agriculture is a vital one for the eighties. And there is no doubt that there is a role and a responsibility for those who retire to the countryside to make their experience and abilities available voluntarily.

People with good business experience may often be able to make a crucial difference to the quality, the range and the viability of rural training schemes. Undoubtedly they have a great deal to offer to initiatives making use of the government's Community Programme.

The Community Programme

These programmes, although they will have to change and evolve, will continue to be used locally in urban or rural areas. The sensitivity and the professionalism with which they are used will determine how effective they are in stimulating the growth of jobs and the generation of new wealth.

What is the Community Programme? It is a Manpower Services Commission scheme aiming to give 130,000 temporary jobs to unemployed people. Their work can be on any project benefiting their communities, from making parks out of derelict sites, and building workshops to creating new allotments. Individuals as well as organisations can sponsor these projects under the Community Programme. The sponsor is responsible for managing and administering the scheme and is expected to drum up some extra financial support to cover expenses not covered by the MSC grant.

The projects must be for work which would not otherwise have been done, and must be designed to provide jobs for local people

In the Community

who have been out of work for several months. The MSC pays full time wages to managers and supervisors, reflecting local rates. Wages are paid to workers on the scheme up to a maximum of £60 a week, plus National Insurance contributions. Schemes can be part-time or full-time, depending on the type of work.

The MSC also refunds the cost of overheads, materials and equipment up to a maximum of £440 a year for each place on the scheme.

Here is a list of possible schemes under the Community Programme:

Environmental improvement
1. Drainage, construction of footpaths, and removal of debris in a country park
2. Clearance of canals and footpaths
3. Stabilisation of sand dunes
4. Tree planting to replace dead elms
5. Creation of conservation areas for rare animals and birds
6. Reclamation of disused land for public use in inner city areas
7. Clearing and fencing off derelict areas
8. Conservation of the coastline
9. Roof insulation and draught proofing of publicly owned dwellings

Provision of social amenities
1. Provision of playgrounds in inner city areas
2. Provision of creche facilities for one-parent families
3. Improvement of sports amenities for public use
4. Conversion of a disused building for use as a training workshop
5. Conversion of a warehouse into a community centre
6. Construction of an adventure playground
7. Improvement of buildings and land for a camping site
8. Rebuilding a derelict farmhouse into a youth centre
9. Creation of picnic areas, nature trail, etc
10. Provision of new allotments
11. Creation of a riding school for the disabled
12. Advising senior citizens on how to avoid hypothermia

Work After Work

Social and cultural work
1. Cataloguing of archives
2. Restoration of old farm machinery for museums
3. Display of historical exhibits in museums
4. Interior decorating service for elderly/disabled people
5. Gardening work for the physically handicapped
6. Production of directory of amenities for disabled people
7. Renovation of clothing and furniture for use by social services
8. Educational theatre for children in deprived areas
9. Maintenance of toys and furniture for playschools

As a sponsor of one of these programmes you would be responsible in the same way as an employer, keeping the project running smoothly and keeping financial records, and although there would be paid managers and supervisors you would need to provide overall supervision. Provision must also be made for the health and safety of employees. You may think that as a retired person this would all be just too much. But remember the projects run for a limited amount of time and you could be capable of helping the area in which you live in two ways: providing some new amenity it would never have got normally and, more important, helping men and women who have been out of work for some time and whose confidence needs rebuilding.

If you have an idea for a scheme and want to press ahead with it as a sponsor, you will need to talk it out with a link team in your area. They can be reached via the local Job Centre. The team will give you information about the people unemployed in your area, and will help organise appropriate schemes.

In the Community

FRANK HENDERSON

Age 61
Previous occupation Personnel and financial administration in the Forestry Commission, dealing with control of private woodland grants.
Occupation now Treasurer for Friends of the Earth in Scotland.

The Scottish FOE has 1,289 members and has been involved in a number of campaigns like Save the Otter in Scotland, fighting nuclear waste disposal at the Mullwharchar enquiry, and seal culling in Orkney.

FOE's aims are well known and Mr Henderson says he can co-exist with most of them although 'I'm not totally won over to them all,' he admits, 'so I hope they can cope with a slight heretic working amongst them.

'I'm managing their accounts and I've taken over a fairly hairy set of books. I'm writing them up to show a proper balance of income and expenses. A lot of people have been dabbling with no idea how to account so I have an organisational job to do.

'This is the sort of organisation which could use a little cynical commonsense. I've told them I'd be prepared to give some talks on their behalf about forestry which I'd like to do. Although I've been a career civil servant I am still an outdoor person and I keep in touch with the countryside. I have sympathy for Friends of the Earth, and agree on at least 80 per cent of issues.'

The Scottish Friends, like in the rest of the United Kingdom, are concerned with saving energy and cleaning up the environment. In over twenty areas there are groups which are involved in garden sharing schemes, recycling, home insulation, beach clean-ups, responses to building plans, cycle paths, objections to woodland felling, and the construction of coastal footpaths. It has formed a Pedestrian Action for Scotland to give a better deal for urban pedestrians, turned waste ground in Edinburgh into allotments, fought to keep open the Kilmacolm Railway, and published a Scottish *Eco Cook Book*.

CHAPTER NINE

WHO'S AFRAID OF FUND RAISING?

Making money is an honourable occupation in business, and the more enterprising companies are the ones where everyone in the organization, from tea boy to chairman, has their eyes on its progress up the profit ladder. Why then does the money-making side of the charity business get cold-shouldered by volunteers? Partly, no doubt, because it is called 'fund raising'. This is a problem of image which a good advertising agency might find challenging. At REACH many of the job applicants give a resounding 'no' to the question on their application form: Are you willing to try your hand at fund raising?

One applicant, a retired accountant, went to work for a museum of historical buildings but found to his dismay that it involved developing a plan to attract funding for specific projects by presenting a well prepared case for prospective donors — and identifying those donors in the first place. 'This is fund raising and I definitely didn't want that. It requires a special outlook,' he said.

Hilary Blume, who has written a comprehensive book on fund raising, thinks that everyone in a charity shares some responsibility for raising the money, just as everyone in a factory or business shares a responsibility for its profitability. 'This does not mean each member of staff has to raise a target amount, but they must comport themselves in a way which inspires confidence in the charity's work.'

Fund raising is disagreeable work to many, says Ms Blume. A retired executive going to work for a voluntary group might think — 'I've got to ask my friends for money!' 'But they do not have to be involved in direct asking,' she says. 'They can organise donor records, mount a covenant campaign and provide an administrative back-up to the fund raiser. It is really all about sensible commitment.

Who's Afraid of Fund Raising

You can have someone who is full of new ideas but they may be daft ideas. You need someone with commonsense who can weigh the cost-effectiveness of their ideas.'

A fine example of how a business mind can help a disadvantaged group is the story of Countrywide Workshops. This cannot be labelled as a fund raising venture because Countrywide Workshops maintains jobs for blind and disabled workers. But it shows how a combination of flair and concern can produce practical help for the disabled by turning donors into consumers.

Countrywide Workshops is a mail order business which sells work produced by people at home, and in workshops. Their products are photographed for a catalogue which is sent to potential customers throughout the United Kingdom.

The idea belongs to Valerie Wood-Gaiger, a businesswoman with long experience in marketing. For years she had been raising funds for research into a hereditary form of blindness which affected her family. During 1982 she began to realise that the recession was killing off trade for the blind who made goods for sale. She decided that her selling background should be brought into use to help those workers and other groups of disabled. She gave up her own business and launched into mail order lines:

'I set up Countrywide Workshops not to raise funds for disabled people, but to help maintain their jobs,' she says. The next step is to start a charity to help set up small cottage industries and projects to employ groups of disabled. Eventually the plan is to have a sheltered workshop as part of the mail order business. When Valerie Wood-Gaiger starts fund raising for her charity, it will no doubt be a professional and effective operation.

Fund raising has become a sophisticated business now that big league charities are dealing with yearly sums up to £15 million. This has attracted professional problem-solvers who are an increasingly familiar part of the voluntary sector. Craigmyle and Company has been a consultant to charity for twenty-two years and has helped its clients raise over £170 million. Craigmyle deals in big projects, and whether they can actually be mounted. If a charity brings a proposal to the company its cost-effectiveness and whether it is a runner is assessed. No one can afford to back a loser with such high stakes. 'We have to work out if the administrative cost of the exercise will

Work After Work

take too much of a slice of the final figure,' explains James Bell, Craigmyle's managing director.

'If the costs are 10 per cent or 12 per cent the appeal may not be worth doing. Some charities are happy to pay out up to 20 per cent in administrative costs, but we would not be happy with that figure.'

Mr Bell thinks that a recently retired executive should not be frightened of fund raising. 'Obviously we are dealing with the very big appeals and our staff train for four or five months before going out to help a client, but appeals for local projects can be very rewarding to work for. The public can be very generous if approached well.'

Sending out appeal letters might be the first line of attack of the recently acquired fund raiser but they are often ineffective. 'Duplicate letters in isolation are not a good idea,' adds Mr Bell. 'You have to get the letters right and have some back-up. It is simply no good just mailing out letters and sitting back. This must be part of a whole effort.'

In the past fund raising was seen as something the professionals didn't deal with. Even now volunteers who are keen to be in contact with the people needing help see fund raising as an activity on the fringe of the work — a distraction from the true purpose of the voluntary group. 'It has never been popular,' admits Peter Burns, managing director of the charity consultants Public Voice Communications Ltd. 'Now it has become increasingly more complex. It is like marketing or any other aspect of commerce. In some of the big charities, where the volunteers used to be inveigled into doing it, now it is left to the professionals, to those people who have come in from industry and commerce. It is true that it is more difficult now for an amateur.'

Even so, a new public attitude to giving money is emerging which needs a common touch to exploit. Professional consultants may employ an exact science in tackling how to raise a specific sum — 'they divide the market into blocks of hundreds, seeking, for example, five donations of £10,000,' says Burns. 'You could almost work it out on a graph. I'm not sneering — this is quite legitimate, and I think it is fine for funding buildings but it's no good where people are concerned.'

A growing number of people are showing that they do not want to be passive donors, he says. 'It's no good now simply trying to raise money cold. You have to try to sell the problem to the public. Their attitude is changing and it is not enough to tell them that their money is alleviating symptoms, they want to try to understand the causes of the problem, and you must take heed of this in trying to raise money from them. It's not just a starving child they are giving money for. They want to understand the relationship between the rich and poor countries. I'm not saying that every donor is becoming as discerning as this, but there are a tremendous number of people active in voluntary organisations in this country and their awareness is growing.'

Most of the professionals in the fund raising game agree on one point: to be any good at it you must feel attracted to the work of the charity concerned. Involvement is the key to inspiration. You cannot do it from outside, believes Peter Burns, there has to be commitment. There is no reason why a retired executive can't use his or her wits to put some cash into a scheme which they find appealing and stimulating. 'I learned what I know working in charities,' says Burns, 'so when I retire I could approach REACH and offer my services as a professional fund raiser.'

Useful addresses
Countrywide Workshops, 17c Earls Court Square, London SW5. Tel. 01-373 9943.
Public Voice Communications Ltd., 352 Kennington Road, London SE11. Tel. 01-582 6994.
Craigmyle and Co. Ltd, The Grove, Harpenden, Herts. Tel. 05827-62441.

Reference work
Blume, Hilary, *Fund-Raising: a Comprehensive Handbook*. The Directory of Social Change, 9 Mansfield Place, London NW3. £3.25 (plus 50p post and packing).

This book has been written for those people no longer in careers, jobs, professions. The message is simple. If you think you are finished with work, look around you. The real work is waiting.

APPENDIX A

CLASSIFIED INDEX OF VOLUNTARY GROUPS IN THE UNITED KINGDOM

Addictions
Action on Smoking and Health
Alcoholics Anonymous
Carter Foundation
Federation of Alcoholic Residential
 Establishments
Gamblers Anonymous
National Council on Alcoholism
South Wales Association for Prevention of
 Addiction

Animal welfare
Animal Defence Society
Hawk Trust
National Canine Defence League
People's Dispensary for Sick Animals
Royal Society for the Prevention of Cruelty to
 Animals
Royal Society for the Protection of Birds
World Wildlife Fund

Arts
Amateur Music Association
Art Law Services
Arts Council of Great Britain
British Federation of Music Festivals
British Institute of Recorded Sound
British Society for Music Therapy
British Theatre Association
Central Council for Amateur Theatre
Defence of Literature and Arts Society
English Folk Dance and Song Society
Free Form Arts Trust
Hand Crafts Advisory Association for the
 Disabled
Imperial Society of Teachers of Dancing
Museums Association
Musicians' Benevolent Fund
National Art-Collections Fund
National Operatic and Dramatic Association
Photography for the Disabled
Royal General Theatrical Fund Association
Sesame
Shape
Society for Education Through Art
Women in Media

Benevolent associations
Architects' Benevolent Society
Army Benevolent Fund
Chartered Surveyors' Voluntary Service
Civil Service Benevolent Fund
Coal Industry Social Welfare Organisation
Gardeners' Royal Benevolent Society
Guild of Aid for Gentlepeople
Jewish Aged Needy Pension Society
Musicians' Benevolent Fund
National Benevolent Institution
National Gardens Scheme
Professional Classes Aid Council
Royal Agricultural Benevolent Institution
Royal Air Force Benevolent Fund
Royal General Theatrical Fund Association
Royal Naval Benevolent Trust
Royal United Kingdom Beneficent Association
Solicitors' Benevolent Associations
Teachers' Benevolent Fund

Child Care/Welfare
Association for All Speech Impaired Children
Association of Parents of Vaccine-Damaged
 Children
Dr Barnardo's
Boys' Brigade

Appendix A

British Agencies for Adoption and Fostering
British Association of Early Childhood
 Education
Child Accident Prevention Trust
Child Poverty Action Group
Children's Country Holidays Fund
Children's Legal Centre
Children Need Fathers
Church of England Children's Society
Cot Deaths Research and Support
Crusade of Rescue
Fair Play for Children
Friends of the Children Society
Handicapped Adventure Playground
 Association
Hyperactive Children's Support Group
Infantile Hypercalcaemia Foundation
Invalid Children's Aid Association
Jewish Child's Day
Justice for Children
Lady Hoare Trust for Physically Disabled
 Children
National Adoption Society
National Association for Gifted Children
National Association for Maternal and Child
 Welfare
National Association for the Welfare of Children
 in Hospital
National Childminding Association
National Children's Bureau
National Children's Home
National Council of Voluntary Child Care
 Organisations
National Deaf Children's Society
National Elfrida Rathbone Society
National Foster Care Association
National Society for Autistic Children
National Society for the Prevention of Cruelty to
 Children
Norwood Child Care
Parent to Parent Information on Adoption
 Services
Pre-School Playgroups Association
Royal Society for Mentally Handicapped
 Children and Adults
Sailors' Children's Society
Salvation Army
Save the Children Fund
Shaftesbury Homes and 'Aruthesa'
SOS Children's Villages

Stillbirth and Perinatal Death Association
Toy Libraries Association
Tuberous Sclerosis Association
Twins Clubs Association
Voice of the Child in Care
VOLCUF
Young Family Day Care Association

Churches/Religious organisations
Anglo-Jewish Association
Association of Jewish Refugees in Great Britain
Association for Jewish Youth
Baptist Union of Great Britain and Ireland
Board of Deputies of British Jews
British Council of Churches
Campaigners, The
Catholic Housing Aid Society
Catholic Institute for International Relations
Catholic Marriage Advisory Council
Catholic Men's Society
Catholic Social Service for Prisoners
Catholic Women's League
Catholic Youth Service Council
Central British Fund for World Jewish Relief
Christian Aid
Christian Alliance
Christian Organisations Research and Advisory
 Trust
Church Action on Poverty
Church Army
Church Army Housing
Church of England Board of Education
Church of England Board for Social
 Responsibility
Church of England Children's Society
Church Lads' Brigade
Churches' Council for Health and Healing
Council of Christians and Jews
Crusade of Rescue
Family and Social Action
Fellowship of Reconciliation
Free Church Federal Council
Girls' Friendly Society and Townsend Fellowship
Grail, The
Industrial Christian Fellowship
Jewish Aged Needy Pension Society
Jewish Blind Society
Jewish Child's Day
Jewish Employment Action Group

Work After Work

Jewish Lads' and Girls' Brigade
Jewish Welfare Board
League of Jewish Women
Methodist Church Division of Education and Youth
Methodist Church Division of Social Responsibility
Methodist Homes for the Aged
National Board of Catholic Women
National Christian Education Council
National Council of Young Men's Christian Associations
National Free Church Women's Council
Norwood Child Care
Order of the Orthodox Hospitallers
Religious Society of Friends (Quakers)
Salvation Army
Shaftesbury Society
Social Aid
Social Morality Council
Society of St Vincent de Paul
Sons of Divine Providence
Student Christian Movement
Toc H
Union of Catholic Mothers
Union of Maccabi Associations
Unitarian and Free Christian Churches
United Kingdom Band of Hope
United Reformed Church
Volunteer Missionary Movement
Young Christian Workers
Young Women's Christian Association

Community development
Action Resource Centre
ARVAC (Association of Researchers into Voluntary Action and Community Involvement)
Association for Neighbourhood Councils
British Association of Settlements and Social Action Centres
CETU
Community Projects Foundation
Community Service Volunteers
Community Transport
Family and Social Action
Federation of Community Work Training Groups
Foundation for Alternatives
Inter-Action
International Voluntary Service
National Federation of Community Organisations
Student Community Action Development Unit
West Central Jewish Community Development Centre

Consumer affairs
British Standards Institution
Consumers' Association
Consumers in the European Community Group
Credit Union League of Great Britain
Electricity Consumers' Council
National Association of Citizens Advice Bureaux
National Consumer Council
National Federation of Consumer Groups
National Right to Fuel Campaign

Counselling
Albany Trust
British Association for Counselling
Brook Advisory Centres
Campaign for Homosexual Equality
Catholic Marriage Advisory Council
Compassionate Friends
Counsel and Care for the Elderly
Cruse
National Association of Young People's Counselling and Advisory Services
National Marriage Guidance Council
Parents Anonymous
Pregnancy Advisory Service
Samaritans
SPOD
Westminster Pastoral Foundation
Women's Aid Federation

Education/Training
Advisory Centre for Education
British Association for Early Childhood Education
British Association for Local History
British Council
British Esperanto Association
British ORT
Broadcasting Support Services
Central Bureau for Educational Visits and Exchanges
Centre for World Development Education
CETU

Appendix A

Church of England Board of Education
Committee on Student Placements in Voluntary Agencies
Council for Environmental Conservation
Dyslexia Institute
Educational Centres' Association
Federation of Community Work Training Groups
International Students' Trust
JMB Development Training
Joint University Council for Social and Public Administration
Lingfield Hospital School
Methodist Church Division of Education and Youth
National Adult School Organisation
National Advisory Centre on Careers for Women
National Association for Gifted Children
National Association of Development Education Centres
National Bureau for Handicapped Students
National Christian Education Council
National Confederation of Parent Teacher Associations
National Elfrida Rathbone Association
National Federation of Voluntary Literacy Schemes
National Gypsy Education Council
National Institute of Adult Education
National Union of Students
Queen's Nursing Institute
Residential Colleges Committee
Society for Education Through Art
Student Christian Movement
Thomas Wall Trust
Treloar Trust
Turners Court
United Kingdom Council for Overseas Student Affairs
United Kingdom Home Economics Federation
Universities' Council for Adult Education
Workers' Educational Association

Elderly

Abbeyfield Society
Age Concern
Anchor Housing Association
Centre for Policy on Ageing
Contact
Counsel and Care for the Elderly
Employment Fellowship
Friends of the Elderly and Gentlefolk's Help
Help the Aged
Help the Aged Housing Trust
National Health Service Retirement Fellowship
Pensioners' Voice
Pre-Retirement Association
Retired Executives' Action Clearing House
Sisters of Our Lady of Grace and Compassion
Task Force

Emergency/Relief/Refugees

Asociation of Jewish Refugees in Great Britain
ATD Fourth World
British Refugee Council
British Red Cross Society
Christian Aid
Civil Aid
Committee on South African War Resistance
International Social Service of Great Britain
Medic-Alert Foundation
Ockenden Venture
Order of the Orthodox Hospitallers
Oxfam
Religious Society of Friends
Royal Humane Society
Royal Life Saving Society United Kingdom
Royal National Lifeboat Institution
St John Ambulance
Save the Children Fund
Self Aid of Refugees

Employment/Industry

Action Resource Centre
Apex Trust
Association of Disabled Professionals
Camphill Village Trust
Confederation of British Industry
Co-operative Development Agency
Council for Small Industries in Rural Areas
Development Commission
Employment Fellowship
Equal Pay and Opportunity Campaign
Industrial Common Ownership Movement
Industrial Society
Institute of Personnel Management
Jewish Employment Action Group
Low Pay Unit

Work After Work

National Advisory Centre on Careers for Women
National Joint Committee of Working Women's Organisations
National Unemployment Action Association
Over Forty Association for Women Workers
Pre-Retirement Association
Project Fullemploy
Retired Executives Action Clearing House
Share Community
Social Workers' Pension Fund
Trades Union Congress
United Kingdom Federation of Business and Professional Women
Young Enterprise
Youthaid

Environment/Conservation
Ancient Monuments Society
Architectural Association
British Trust for Conservation Volunteers
Civic Trust
Commons Open Spaces and Footpaths Preservation Society
Commonwealth Human Ecology Council
Conservation Society
Council for Environmental Conservation
Council for Environmental Education
Council for the Protection of Rural England
Countryside Commission
Field Studies Council
Foundation for Alternatives
Friends of the Earth
Green Alliance
Inland Waterways Association
Keep Britain Tidy Group
Men of the Trees
National Heritage
National Housing and Town Planning Council
National Society for Clean Air
National Trust
Natural Environment Research Council
Nature Conservancy Council
Pedestrians' Association
Professional Institutions' Council for Conservation
Ramblers' Association
Rescue
Royal Agricultural Society of England
Royal Institute of British Architects
Royal Society for Nature Conservation
Royal Town Planning Institute
SAVE Britain's Heritage
Society for the Protection of Ancient Buildings
Standing Conference of Rural Community Councils
Streetwork
Town and Country Planning Association
World Wildlife Fund

Equal opportunity
Campaign for Homosexual Equality
Commission for Racial Equality
Equal Opportunities Commission
Equal Pay & Opportunity Campaign
Fawcett Society
National Council of Women
UK Federation of Business and Professional Women

Family/Parental welfare
Association for Improvements in the Maternity Services
Association of Parents of Vaccine-Damaged Children
British Organisation of Non-Parents
Child Poverty Action Group
Children Need Fathers
Contact a Family
Cope
Fairbridge Society
Families Need Fathers
Family Forum
Family Rights Group
Family Service Units
Family and Social Action
Family Welfare Association
Gingerbread
Maternity Alliance
Meet-a-Mum Association
Mothers' Union
National Association for the Childless
National Association for Maternal and Child Welfare
National Childbirth Trust
National Council for Carers and their Elderly Dependants
National Council for the Divorced and Separated
National Council for One-Parent Families
National Marriage Guidance Council

Appendix A

Organisation for Parents Under Stress
Parent to Parent Information on Adoption Services
Parents Anonymous
Society to Support Home Confinements
Study Commission on the Family
Young Family Day Care Association

Family planning

Birth Control Campaign
Birth Control Trust
British Pregnancy Advisory Service
Brook Advisory Centres
Family Planning Association
Pregnancy Advisory Service

Grant-making trusts/ Foundations

Barrow and Geraldine S Cadbury Trust
Calouste Gulbenkian Foundation
Carnegie United Kingdom Trust
Hilden Charitable Fund
Joseph Rowntree Memorial Trust
King George's Jubilee Trust
Nuffield Foundation
Pilgrim Trust
Royal Jubilee Trusts
Sainsbury Family Charitable Trusts
Sir Halley Stewart Trust
Thomas Wall Trust
Wolfson Foundation

Health/Handicap

Disablement (general)
Association of Disabled Professionals
Association for Independent Disabled Self-Sufficiency
Association of Parents of Vaccine-Damaged Children
Centre on Environment for the Handicapped
Contact a Family
Disability Alliance
Disabled Drivers' Motor Club
Disabled International Visits Exchange
Disabled Living Foundation
Disablement Income Group
Disablement Information Advice Line
Gardens for the Disabled Trust

Hand Crafts Advisory Association for the Disabled
Handicapped Adventure Playground Association
Horticultural Therapy
Invalid Children's Aid Association
Invalids at Home
John Groom's Association for the Disabled
Lady Hoare Trust for Physically Disabled Children
Mobility Information Service
Mobility International
Motability
National Bureau for Handicapped Students
National Federation of St Raphael Clubs
National Fund for Research into Crippling Diseases
Outset
PHAB
Photography for the Disabled
Queen Elizabeth's Foundation for the Disabled
Royal Association for Disability and Rehabilitation
Sesame
Share Community
SPOD
Talking Books for the Handicapped
Treloar Trust
Wider Horizons
Wireless for the Bedridden

Physical Handicaps
Association for All Speech-Impaired Children
Association for Research into Restricted Growth
Association for Stammerers
Back Pain Association
Breakthrough Trust
British Association of the Hard of Hearing
British Deaf Association
British Limbless Ex-Servicemen's Association
Commonwealth Society for the Deaf
Council for Hearing Impaired Visits and Exchanges
Guide Dogs for the Blind Association
Incorporated Association for Promoting the General Welfare of the Blind
Jewish Blind Society
National Deaf-Blind Helpers' League
National Deaf Children's Society
National Library for the Blind

Work After Work

Partially Sighted Society
Royal Association in Aid of the Deaf and Dumb
Royal Commonwealth Society for the Blind
Royal National Institute for the Blind
Royal National Institute for the Deaf
St Dunstans for Men and Women Blinded on War Service
'Stylopal' Braille Pen Pal Club

Mental Illness/Handicap
Anorexic Aid
Campaign for Mentally Handicapped People
Camphill Village Trust
Depressives Associated
Ex-Services' Mental Welfare Society
Mental After-Care Association
Mental Health Foundation
National Association for Mental Health
National Federation of Gateway Clubs
National Schizophrenia Fellowship
National Society for Autistic Children
One to One
Open Door Association
Path
Psychiatric Rehabilitation Association
Richmond Fellowship
Royal Society for Mentally Handicapped Children and Adults
Society of Analytical Psychology

Specific Maladies
Action for Research into Multiple Sclerosis
Alzheimer's Disease Society
Anorexic Aid
Arthritis and Rheumatism Council
Association to Combat Huntington's Chorea
Association for Spina Bifida and Hydrocephalus
Asthma Research Council
British Diabetic Association
British Dyslexia Association
British Epilepsy Association
British Heart Foundation
British Migraine Association
British Polio Fellowship
British Retinitis Pigmentosa Society
British Tinnitus Association
Brittle Bone Society
Cancer Relief
Cancer Research Campaign
Cardiac Spare Parts Club
Chest, Heart & Stroke Association

Coeliac Society
Colostomy Welfare Group
Cystic Fibrosis Research Trust
Dyslexia Institute
Friedreich's Ataxia Group
Haemophilia Society
Hyperactive Children's Support Group
Ileostomy Association
Infantile Hypercalcaemia Foundation
International Glaucoma Association
Lepra
Leukaemia Research Fund
Leukaemia Society
Mastectomy Association
Migraine Trust
Motor Neurone Disease Society
Multiple Sclerosis Society
Muscular Dystrophy Group
National Ankylosing Spondylitis Society
National Association for Deaf-Blind and Rubella Handicapped
National Association of Laryngectomee Clubs
National Eczema Society
National Federation of Kidney Patients Associations
National Schizophrenia Fellowship
National Society for Autistic Children
National Society for Epilepsy
Parkinson's Disease Society
Renal Society
Spastics' Society
Spinal Injuries Association
Tuberous Sclerosis Association
Women's National Cancer Control Campaign

Institutional/Community Health
Action on Smoking and Health
Association of Community Health Councils for England and Wales
Association for Improvements in the Maternity Services
British Acupuncture Association
British Association of Dramatherapists
British Association of Occupational Therapists
British Hospitals Contributory Schemes Association
British Library of Tape Recordings for Hospital Patients
British Medical Association
British Red Cross Society

Appendix A

Chartered Society of Physiotherapy
Churches' Council for Health and Healing
Community Health Group for Ethnic Minorities
Eugenics' Society
Foundation for the Study of Infant Deaths
Health Education Council
Health Visitors' Association
Hospital Saving Association
Joint Committee Order of St John and British Red Cross
King's Fund Centre
Leonard Cheshire Foundation
Marie Curie Memorial Foundation
Medic-Alert Foundation
Mid-Life Centre
Most Venerable Order of the Hospital of St John of Jerusalem
National Association of Leagues of Hospital Friends
National Association for the Welfare of Children in Hospital
Patients' Association
Queen's Nursing Institute
Royal College of Midwives
Royal College of Nursing
Royal Institute of Public Health and Hygiene
Royal Society of Health
Royal Society of Medicine
Royal Society for Prevention of Accidents
St John Ambulance
Servite Houses
Socialist Health Association
Society of Community Medicine
South Wales Association for Prevention of Addiction
Sue Ryder Foundation
Voluntary Euthanasia Society

Housing/Residential care
Abbeyfield Society
Anchor Housing Association
Dr Barnardo's
British Limbless Ex-Servicemen's Association
Camphill Village Trust
Carr-Gomm Society Ltd
Catholic Housing Aid Society
Cecil Homes
CHAR (Campaign for Homeless Single People)
Christian Alliance
Church Army Housing
Church of England Children's Society
Distressed Gentlefolk's Aid Association
Douglas Haig Memorial Homes
Federation of Alcoholic Residential Establishments
Forces' Help Society and Lord Roberts' Workshops
Griffins' Society
Help the Aged
Housing Associations' Charitable Trust
Housing Centre Trust
Housing Corporation
Institute of Housing
John Groom's Association for the Disabled
Leonard Cheshire Foundation
Mental After Care Association
Methodist Homes for the Aged
National Association of Almshouses
National Association of Voluntary Hostels
National Children's Home
National Cyrenians
National Federation of Housing Associations
National Housing and Town Planning Council
National Tenants' Organisation
Over Forty Association for Women Workers
Residential Care Association
Richmond Fellowship
Servite Houses
SHAC (London Housing Aid Centre)
Shaftesbury Homes and 'Arethusa'
Shaftesbury Society
Shelter
Shelter National Housing Aid Trust
Sisters of Our Lady of Grace and Compassion
Society of St Vincent de Paul
SOS Society
Stoneham Housing Association
Sue Ryder Foundation
Women's Aid Federation

Human rights
Amnesty International
Anti-Apartheid Movement
Anti-Slavery Society for the Protection of Human Rights
British Institute of Human Rights
Committee on South African War Resistance
Fellowship of Reconciliation
Minority Rights Group
National Council for Civil Liberties

Work After Work

National Peace Council
Pax Christi
Peace Pledge Union
United Nations Association
Women's International League for Peace and Freedom
Writers' and Scholars' Educational Trust

Information services

Association of Charity Officers
Association of Land-Owning Charities
Charities Aid Foundation
Community Transport
Consumers' Association
Councils for Voluntary Service — National Association
Disability Alliance
Disabled Living Foundation
Inter-Action
Joint Council for the Welfare of Immigrants
King's Fund Centre
Legislation Monitoring Service for Charities
Mobility Information Service
National Advisory Centre on Careers for Women
National Association of Citizens' Advice Bureaux
National Council for Civil Liberties
National Council for Voluntary Organisations
National Federation of Consumer Groups
Parent to Parent Information on Adoption Services
Plunkett Foundation
Runnymede Trust
Rural Voice
SHAC (London Housing Aid Centre)
Shelter
Standing Conference of Rural Community Councils
Standing Conference of Women's Organisations
United Kingdom Immigrants' Advisory Service
Volunteer Centre

International

Action Aid
Amnesty International
ATD Fourth World
British ORT
British Volunteer Programme
Brothers to All Men
Catholic Institute for International Relations
Centre for World Development Education
Christian Aid
Commonwealth Countries' League
Commonwealth Human Ecology Council
Commonwealth Society for the Deaf
Council for Hearing Impaired Visits and Exchanges
Disabled International Visits Exchange
Intermediate Technology Development Group
International Friendship League
International Glaucoma Association
International Social Service of Great Britain
International Students' Trust
International Voluntary Service
Mobility International
National Council for Welfare of Prisoners Abroad
Ockenden Venture
Oxfam
Project Trust
Returned Volunteer Action
Rotary International
Royal Commonwealth Society for the Deaf
SOS Children's Villages
Third World First
United Nations Association
Voluntary Service Overseas
Volunteer Missionary Movement
War on Want
Women's International League for Peace and Freedom
World-wide Education Service of PNEU
World University Service

Law/Justice

Artlaw
Association of Land-owning Charities
Children's Legal Centre
Association of Magisterial Officers
Central Council of Magistrates' Courts, Committees
Family Rights Group
Justice for Children
Law Society
Legal Action Group
Legislation Monitoring Service for Charities
Magistrates' Association
National Council for Civil Liberties
Rights of Women
Senate of the Inns of Court and the Bar

Appendix A

Local government/Public administration
Association of County Councils
Association of District Councils
Association of Local Authorities of Northern Ireland
Association of Metropolitan Authorities
Convention of Scottish Local Authorities
Institute of Local Government
National Association of Local Councils
Rating and Valuation Association
Royal Institute of Public Administration
Society of Local Authority Chief Executives

Management
Association of Charity Officers
British Institute of Management
British Institute of Management Foundation
Christian Organisations' Research and Advisory Trust
Industrial Society
Women in Management

Maritime/Seafarers
Apostleship of the Sea
British Sailors' Society
Marine Society
Missions to Seamen
Royal Alfred Seafarers' Society
Royal National Lifeboat Institution
Royal National Mission to Deep Sea Fishermen
Sailors' Children's Society
Sea Cadet Corps

Minority groups
Community Health Group for Ethnic Minorities
Joint Council for the Welfare of Immigrants
Minority Rights Group
National Association for Asian Youth
National Association of Community Relations Councils
National Gypsy Education Council
Runnymede Trust
United Kingdom Immigrants' Advisory Service
Westindian Concern

Offenders
Apex Trust
Catholic Social Service for Prisoners
Griffins' Society
Howard League
Institute for the Study and Treatment of Delinquency
NACRO (National Association for the Care and Resettlement of Offenders)
National Association of Prison Visitors
National Association of Probation Officers
National Association of Victims' Support Schemes
National Council for Welfare of Prisoners Abroad
Police Federation of England and Wales
Prison Officers' Association
Prison Reform Trust
Rainer Foundation
Society of Voluntary Associates

Recreation
British Library of Tape Recordings for Hospital Patients
Camping and Caravanning Club
Central Council of Physical Recreation
Children's Country Holidays Fund
Countrywide Holidays Association
Disabled Drivers' Motor Club
Duke of Edinburgh's Award
Fair Play for Children
Farm Women's Club
Festival Welfare Services
Gardens for the Disabled Trust and Garden Club
Handicapped Adventure Playground Association
HF Holidays
Keep Fit Association
National Federation of Gateway Clubs
National Federation of Young Farmers' Clubs
National Playing Fields Association
National Society of Allotment and Leisure Gardeners
Outward Bound Trust
Photography for the Disabled
Ramblers' Association
Sports Council
'Stylopal' Braille Pen Pal Club
Sundial Society
Talking Books for the Handicapped
Toy Libraries Association
Wider Horizons
Wireless for the Bedridden
Working Men's Club and Institute Union
Youth Hostels Association

Work After Work

Research
Action for Research into Multiple Sclerosis
Alzheimer's Disease Society
Arthritis & Rheumatism Council
ARVAC
Association to Combat Huntington's Chorea
Association for Research into Restricted Growth
Asthma Research Council
Back Pain Association
British Dyslexia Association
British Society for Social Responsibility in Science
Brittle Bone Society
Cancer Research Campaign
Christian Organisations' Research and Advisory Trust
Cot Deaths Research and Support
Council for Science and Society
Cystic Fibrosis Research Trust
Dyslexia Institute
Eugenics' Society
Friedreich's Ataxia Group
Infantile Hypercalcaemia Foundation
Institute of Social Welfare
Institute for the Study and Treatment of Delinquency
Leukaemia Research Fund
Low Pay Unit
Marie Curie Memorial Foundation
Mental Health Foundation
Medical Research Council
Migraine Trust
Multiple Sclerosis Society
Muscular Dystrophy Group
National Children's Bureau
National Fund for Research into Crippling Diseases
National Schizophrenia Fellowship
National Youth Bureau
Policy Studies Institute
Science Research Council
Social Research Association
Social Science Research Council
Socialist Health Association
Society of Analytical Psychology
Society for Co-operative Studies
Study Commission on the Family
Tavistock Institute of Human Relations
Tavistock Institute of Medical Psychology
Tuberous Sclerosis Association
Women's Research and Resources Centre

Rural
Associated Country Women of the World
Council for the Preservation of Rural England
Farm Women's Club
Institute of Rural Life
National Federation of Women's Institutes
National Federation of Young Farmers' Clubs
Plunkett Foundation
Rural Voice
Standing Conference of Rural Community Councils

Self-help
Alcoholics Anonymous
Anorexic Aid
Association for Research into Restricted Growth
Association for Self-Help and Community Groups
Breakthrough Trust
British Polio Fellowship
British Tinnitus Association
Campaign for Homosexual Equality
Colostomy Welfare Group
Contact a Family
Depressives Associated
Gamblers Anonymous
Gingerbread
Mastectomy Association
Mid-Life Centre
National Association of Victims' Support Schemes
National Federation of Kidney Patients' Association
National Unemployment Action Association
Open Door Association
Organisation for Parents under Stress
Royal Society for Mentally Handicapped Children and Adults
Share Community
Tuberous Sclerosis Association
Twins' Clubs' Association

Service, ex-service
Air Training Corps
Army Benevolent Fund
Army Cadet Force Association
British Limbless Ex-Servicemen's Association
Council of Voluntary Welfare Work

Appendix A

Douglas Haig Memorial Homes
Ex-Services' Mental Welfare Society
Forces' Help Society and Lord Roberts' Workshops
League of Remembrance
'Not-Forgotten' Association
Royal British Legion
Royal Naval Benevolent Trust
Soldiers', Sailors' and Airmens' Families Association

Social/Community work
Association of Community Workers
Association of Directors of Social Services
British Association of Social Workers
British Union of Social Workers
Central Council for Education and Training in Social Work
Community and Youth Workers' Union
Institute of Home Help Organisers
Institute of Welfare Officers
National Association of Chief Education Social Workers
National Association of Social Workers in Education
National Institute for Social Work

Social Service
Association of Inner Wheel Clubs
Councils for Voluntary Service — National Association
National Association of Round Tables
Rotary International
Social Aid
Toc H
Voluntary Social Aid
Women's Royal Voluntary Service

Voluntary sector development
ARVAC
Charity Commission
Councils for Voluntary Service — National Association
National Council for Voluntary Organisations
Northern Ireland Council of Social Service
Scottish Council of Social Service
Voluntary Services' Unit
Volunteer Centre
Wales Council for Voluntary Action

Women
Associated Country Women of the World
Association for Improvements in the Maternity Services
Association of Inner Wheel Clubs
British Federation of University Women
British Pregnancy Advisory Service
Catholic Women's League
Commonwealth Countries' League
Co-operative Women's Guild
Electrical Association for Women
Equal Pay and Opportunity Campaign
Farm Women's Club
Fawcett Society
Griffins' Society
Josephine Butler Society
Keep Fit Association
League of Jewish Women
Medical Women's Federation
Mothers' Union
National Advisory Centre on Careers for Women
National Association of Widows
National Association of Women Citizens
National Association of Women Pharmacists
National Association of Women's Clubs
National Board of Catholic Women
National British Women's Total Abstinence Union
National Childbirth Trust
National Council of Women
National Federation of Women's Institutes
National Free Church Women's Council
National Housewives Register
National Joint Committee of Working Women's Organisations
National Union of Townswomen's Guilds
Over Forty Association for Women Workers
Pregnancy Advisory Service
Rights of Women
Royal British Legion Women's Section
Sequel
Society to Support Home Confinements
Soroptimist International of Great Britain and Ireland
Standing Conference of Women's Organisations
United Kingdom Federation of Business and Professional Women
Women's Aid Federation
Women's Farm and Garden Association

Work After Work

Women's Gas Federation and Young Homemakers
Women's International League for Peace and Freedom
Women's League of Health and Beauty
Women in Management
Women in Media
Women's National Cancer Control Campaign
Women's National Commission
Women's Research and Resources Centre
Women's Royal Voluntary Service
Women's Solid Fuel Council

Youth

Air Training Corps
Army Cadet Force Association
Association for Jewish Youth
Boys' Brigade
British Youth Council
Church Lads' and Church Girls' Brigade
Community Service Volunteers
Duke of Edinburgh's Award
Girl Guides' Association
Girls' Brigade
Girls' Friendly Society and Townsend Fellowship
Girls' Venture Corps
Home Base
Jewish Lads' and Girls' Brigade
JMB Development Training
London Youth Advisory Centre
Methodist Church Division of Education and Youth
National Association for Asian Youth
National Association of Boys' Clubs
National Association of Young People in Care
National Association of Young People's Counselling and Advisory Services
National Association of Youth Clubs
National Council for Voluntary Youth Services
National Council of Young Men's Christian Associations
National Federation of 18+ Groups
National Federation of Young Farmers' Clubs
National Playing Fields Association
National Union of Students
National Youth Bureau
Outward Bound Trust
Project Trust
Royal Jubilee Trusts
Scout Association
Sea Cadets' Corps
Turner's Court
Young Christian Workers
Young Enterprise
Young Women's Christian Association
Youthaid
Youth Hostels' Association

APPENDIX B

INDEX OF ESTABLISHED ENTERPRISE AGENCIES

The agencies are sponsored by big and small companies alike, ranging from Barclays Bank, GEC Telecom, Unilever, Whitbread, Marks and Spencer, Mullard, Thorn EMI, ICI Pharmaceuticals, to local firms, universities, chambers of commerce, borough councils and radio stations. A Directory detailing the companies and organisations supporting each agency is available from Business in the Community, 227a City Road, London EC1V 1JU. Tel. 01-253 3716.

North region

Cleveland	Cleveland Enterprise Agency 52/60 Corporation Road Middlesbrough Cleveland TS1 2RW **Director** George Brown *Telephone* 0642-222836	**Darlington**	Darlington & S W Durham Business Venture Imperial Centre Grange Road Darlington **Director** Cyril Beere *Telephone* 0325 480891
Consett	Derwentside Industrial Development Agency Berry Edge Road Consett Co. Durham **Chief Executive** Laurie Haveron *Telephone:* 0207-509124	**Hartlepool**	Hartlepool Enterprise Agency Ltd 5th Floor Titan House York Road Hartlepool **Director** Alan Humble *Telephone:* 0429-221216

143

Work After Work

North East	Enterprise North Durham University Business School Mill Lane Durham **Co-ordinator** Derek Craven *Telephone* 0385 41919	**Bolton**	Bolton Business Venture Bolton Centre Lower Bridgeman Street Bolton **Director** R. McMullan
Northumberland	Business for Cumberland Southgate Morpeth NE63 2EH *Telephone:* 0670 514343	**Bury**	Bury Enterprise Centre 12 Tythebarn Street Bury Lancashire *Telephone* 061 797 5864
Tyne & Wear	Tyne & Wear Enterprise Trust Ltd (Entrust) SWS House Stoddart Street Newcastle-upon-Tyne NE2 1AN **Director** John Eversley *Telephone* 0632 614464	**Ellesmere Port & Neston**	Entep Trust Ltd 118 Whitby Road Ellesmere Port South Wirral **General Manager** C. D. Leatherbarrow *Telephone* 051 356 3555

North West region

Birkenhead/Wirral	In Business Ltd Small Business Centre Claughton Road Birkenhead Wirral Merseyside **Director** Paul Farrow *Telephone* 051 647 7574	**Hyndburn**	Hyndburn Enterprise Trust c/o GEC, Blackburn Road Clayton-le-Moors Accrington Lancashire BB5 5JW **Director** H. Patterson *Telephone* 0254 33241
		Lancaster	Business for Lancaster St Leonards House (Room B32) St Leonards Gate Lancaster **Director** Peter Stiles *Telephone* 0524 66222
Blackburn	Blackburn and District Enterprise Agency c/o Kenyon Bakeries & Caterers Crossfield Street Blackburn **Director** J. Clarke *Telephone* 0254-554945	**Liverpool**	Business in Liverpool Ltd The Innovation Centre 131 Mount Pleasant Liverpool L3 5TF **Director** L. T. Williams *Telephone* 051 709 1231

Appendix

Macclesfield Macclesfield Business Venture
c/o Josolyne & Co
Silk House
Park Green
Macclesfield
Cheshire
Director
John Rosthorn
Telephone
0625-28011

Manchester Manchester Business Venture
Tootals Ltd
56 Oxford Street
Manchester M60 1HJ
Director
Jim MacDonald
Telephone
061 228 1144

Oldham Business in Oldham
Cairo Mill
Waterhead
Oldham OL4 3JA
Director
Roy Newton
Telephone
061-665 1225
061-624 0281 extn. 262

Rochdale Metropolitan Enterprise Trust
Rochdale Area (METRA)
TBA Industrial Products Ltd
PO Box 40
Rochdale OL12 7EQ
Chairman
Robert H. Pearce
Telephone
0706 356250

Rossendale Rossendale Enterprise Trust Ltd
29 Kay Street
Rawtenstall
Rossendale
Lancashire BB4 7LS
Director
Roger Pearson
Telephone
0706 229838

Southport Sefton Enterprise Trust
54 West Street
Southport
Lancashire
Director
Douglas Anderson
Telephone
0704 44173

St Helens Community of St Helens Trust
PO Box 36
St Helens
Merseyside
Director
David Boult
Telephone
0744 692570

Tameside Tameside Venture Trust
Mercian House
Mercian Way
Ashton-under-Lyme
Director
R. Crawshaw
Telephone
061-344 3407

Vale Royal Vale Royal Small Firms Ltd
The Mid-Cheshire Business Centre
Winnington Avenue
Winnington
Northwich
Cheshire CW8 4EE
General Manager
J. B. Bone
Telephone
0606 77711

Warrington Warrington Business Promotion Bureau
Barbauld House
Barbauld Street
Warrington WA1 2QY
Director
Brian Rick
Telephone
0925 33309

145

Work After Work

Widnes/ Runcorn	Business Link 62 Church Street Runcorn Cheshire **Director** B W Burton *Telephone* 092 85 63037	**Hull**	Action Resource Centre Hull Business Advice Centre 24 Anlaby Road Hull HU1 2PA **Contact** Humberside Manager Tony Spice *Telephone* 0482 27266
Wigan	Wigan New Enterprise Ltd 11 Bridgeman Terrace Wigan WN1 1SZ **Managing Director** Paul Davidson *Telephone* 0492 496591	**Leeds**	Leeds Business Venture 4th Floor Merrion House The Merrion Centre Leeds LS2 8LY **Director** Mike Walker *Telephone* 0532 446474 0532 457583
Workington	Moss Bay Enterprise Trust (MOBET) MOBET Trading Estate Workington Cumbria **Chairman** Max de Redder **Manager** A Winterbottom *Telephone* 0900 65656	**Rotherham**	Rotherham Enterprise Agency Ltd Guardian Centre Rotherham South Yorks S6 5DD **Executive Director** George Linney *Telephone* 0709 212 extn. 3463

Yorkshire and Humberside region

Grimsby	Great Grimsby Small Firms Advisory Bureau Devonshire House Grimsby **Contacts** John Robertson Mel Pretious *Telephone* 0472 59161 (Grimsby) 0472 696111 (Cleethorpes)	**Sheffield**	Sheffield Business Venture 32 Collegiate Crescent Sheffield S10 2BJ **Director** Brian Perkins *Telephone* 0742 666471
Halifax	Calderdale Small Business Advice Centre 4 Clare Road Halifax **Director** Ron Chandler *Telephone* 0422 69487	**Wakefield and Kirklees**	Kirklees and Wakefield Venture Trust 12 Rishworth Street Wakefield WF1 3BY and Commerce House New North Road Huddersfield HD1 5PJ **Director** Lou Mullins *Telephone* 0924 381343 and 0484 31352

Appendi.

York Vale of York Small
 Business Association
 Lower Friargate
 York YO1 1SL
 Director
 Gil Elliott
 Telephone
 0904 641401

West Midland region

Birmingham Birmingham Venture
 Chamber of Commerce House
 PO Box 360
 75 Harborne Road
 Birmingham
 Manager
 Graham Ashmore
 Telephone
 021 454 6171

Coventry Coventry Business Centre
 Ground Floor
 Spire House
 New Union Street
 Coventry CV1 2PN
 Manager
 Alan Kimberley
 Telephone
 0203 552781

Stoke/Staffs Business Initiative
 Gordon Chambers
 36 Cheapside
 Hanley
 Stoke on Trent
 Director
 Chris Stokoe
 Telephone
 0782 279013

Telford The Shropshire Enterprise Trust
 Nat West Bank Chambers
 Church Street
 Wellington
 Shropshire
 Director
 R. Brinley Williams
 Telephone
 0952-56624

Walsall Walsall Small Firms Advice Unit
 Jerome Chambers
 Bridge Street
 Walsall WS1 1EX
 Director
 Frank Cookson
 Telephone
 0922-646614

Wolver- Wolverhampton Enterprise Ltd
hampton Lich Chambers
 44 Queen Square
 Wolverhampton
 Director
 Jane Gilbert
 (Coopers & Lybrand,
 funded by Wolverhampton
 Corporation)
 Telephone
 0902 23104

East Midlands region

Chesterfield Chesterfield (ARC)
 Business Advice Centre
 34 Beetwell Street
 Chesterfield
 Derbyshire
 S40 1SH
 Manager
 Robert Taylor
 Telephone
 0246 208743

Corby Corby Business Advisory Bureau
 Douglas House
 37 Queen Square
 Corby
 Northants
 Manager
 L C Howard
 Telephone
 05366 62571

Derby Derby & Derbyshire Business
  Venture
 Saxon House
 Heritage Gate
 Friary Street
 Derby DE1 1NL
 Executive Director
 Michael C. Powell

147

Work After Work

Leicester	Leicestershire Business Venture Business Advice Centre 30 New Walk Leicester LE1 6TF **Director** John Cutler *Telephone* 0533 554464
Melton Mowbray	MIDAS (Melton Industrial Development Aid Scheme) c/o Petfoods Melton Mowbray Leicestershire **Director** Don Hodgson *Telephone* 0664 60006
Northampton	INPUT (Northamptonshire Industrial Promotion Unit) 65 The Avenue Cliftonville Northants **Director** Alan McKay *Telephone* 0604 37401
Nottingham	Nottinghamshire Business Venture c/o John Players Nottingham NG7 5PY **Director** Ian Bulloch *Telephone* 0602 787711

Eastern region

Braintree	BEES Enterprise Office Town Hall Centre Market Square Braintree Essex CM7 6Y6 **Adviser** Stuart Beckwith **Secretary** Carol Marshall *Telephone* 0376 43140
Colchester	Colchester Business Enterprise Agency Gate House High Street Colchester Essex **Director** Peter Taylor *Telephone* 0206 48833
Great Yarmouth	Great Yarmouth Business Advisory Service 165a King Street, Great Yarmouth Norfolk NR30 2PA **Liaison Officer** John Norton *Telephone* 0493 58157
Harlow	Harlow Enterprise Agency c/o Town Hall The High Harlow Essex CM20 1HJ **Liaison Officer** David Ross *Telephone* 0279 446002

Appendix b

Ipswich Ipswich Enterprise Trust
(IPSENTA)
30a Lower Brooke Street
Ipswich
Suffolk
Director
David Rolfe
Telephone
0473 59832

Letchworth Letchworth Enterprise
Letchworth Garden City Corp
Estate Office
Broadway
Letchworth
Herts
Adviser
Rupert Gurney
Telephone
04626 5211

Lowestoft Lowestoft Enterprise Trust
All Saints Road
Pakefield
Lowestoft
Suffolk
NR33 0JL
Director
Chris Barnes
Telephone
0502 63286

Luton BECENTA
(Bedfordshire & Chiltern
Enterprise Agency)
Enterprise House
7 Gordon Street
Luton
LU1 2QP
Director
Derek Upcott
Telephone
0582 452288
also available at
0494 782903

Norwich NEAT
(Norwich Enterprise
Agency Trust)
112 Barrack Street
Norwich NR3 1TX
Director
Bill Page
Telephone
0603 613023

Peterborough Peterborough Enterprise
Programme
Broadway Court
Broadway
Peterborough PE1 1RP
Director
John Duckworth
Telephone
0733 310159

Stevenage Stevenage Initiative
Daneshill House
Danestrete
Stevenage
Herts
Advice Centre Manager
Fred Tippler
Telephone
0438 56117

Wisbech Fens Business Enterprise Trust
2 York Row
Wisbech
Cambridgeshire
Director
Ron Wheeler
Telephone
0945 587084

South Eastern region

Aldershot/ Blackwater Valley Enterprise
Frimley Trust
6 Gordon Road
Aldershot
Hants
Director
Walter Oakey
Telephone
0252 319272

Work After Work

Ashford Enterprise Ashford
28 North Street
Ashford
Kent
Director
Alan Duncan
Telephone
0233 30307

Basingstoke Basingstoke & Andover
Enterprise Centre
Hubbard Road
Basingstoke
RG21 2TY
Director
Bernard Affleck
Telephone
0256 54041

Berkshire Berkshire Enterprise Agency
The Old Shire Hall
The Forbury
Reading
Director
Ansel Harris
Telephone
0734 58715

Gravesham Gravesham Industry Ltd
The Civic Centre
Gravesend
Kent
Secretary
Ron Dewar
Telephone
0474 64422 extn. 274

Isle of Wight Isle of Wight Enterprise Trust Ltd
6/7 Town Lane
Newport
Isle of Wight
PO30 1NR
Director
Ron Neve
Telephone
0983 529 120

Maidstone Maidstone Enterprise Agency
25A Pudding Lane
Maidstone
Kent
Director
John Lee
Telephone
0622 675547

Medway Medway Enterprise Agency
Railway Street
Chatham
Kent ME4 4RR
Director
Guy Sibley MBE
Telephone
0634 43201

Portsmouth The Portsmouth Area Enterprise
1st Floor
27 Guildhall Walk
Portsmouth
Hants
Director
Bill Sumner
Telephone
0705 833321

Southampton Southampton Enterprise Agency
57a Winchester Road
Southampton SO1 5RL
Director
John Townsent
Telephone
0703 788088

Swale SWIM
(Swale Work Initiation Measure)
and SWAP
(Swale Workshop Action Project)
Newington Enterprise Centre
Hardwell Lane
Newington
Sittingbourne
Kent ME10 3RT
Chief Executive
Bill Penney
Telephone
0795 843802

Appendix B

South West region

Bristol
Aid to Bristol Enterprises (ABE)
16 Clifton Park
Bristol BS8 3BY
Co-Directors
Paul Cotterill
Donald Weeks
Telephone
0272 741518

East Devon
East Devon
    Small Industries Group
115 Border Road
Heath Park
Honiton
Devon
EX14 8BT
Development Officer
Albert Johnson
Telephone
0404 41806

Gloucestershire
Gloucestershire Enterprise
    Agency
90 Westgate Street
Gloucester
GL1 2N2
Director
Jack Tester
Telephone
0452 501411

Kingswood (Bristol)
New Work Trust Co Ltd
Avondale Workshops
Woodland Way
Kingswood
Bristol
BS15 1QH
Managing Director
Michael G. Winwood
Telephone
0272 603871

Mid Cornwall
Mid Cornwall Industrial Group
c/o Co-operative Retail
    Services Ltd
2 Fore Street
Bodmin
Cornwall
Telephone
0208 5457

Plymouth
The South Hams Small
    Industries Group
The Croft
Brixton
Plymouth
Devon
Director
Alan Lovering
(Co-Ordinator)
Telephone
0752 880210

Restormel (Mid Cornwall)
Restormel Local Enterprise
    Trust Ltd
Lower Penarwyn
St Blazey
Par
Nr St Austell
Cornwall
Honorary Director
A G Tourell
Telephone
072 681 3079

Swindon
Swindon Enterprise Trust
1 Commercial Road
Swindon
Wilts
Director
Robert Hardy
Telephone
0793 487793

West Cornwall (Kerrier, Penwith & Carrick)
West Cornwall Enterprise
    Trust Ltd
Wesley Street
Camborne
Cornwall
Director
Philip S Staton
Telephone
0209 714914

West Somerset Sedgemoor
Small Industries Group
    Somerset
Dunwear Bungalow
River Lane
Dunwear
Bridgwater
Somerset TA7 0AA
Director
Fred Wedlake MBE
Telephone
0278 424459

Work After Work

London region

Brixton
Brixton United
Coldharbour Works
245a Coldharbour Lane
Brixton
London
SW9
Director
Tony Prendergast
Telephone
01-274 7700 extn. 34

Greenwich
The Thames Enterprise Agency Ltd
Penhall Road
Charlton
London SE7
Manager
C Barrow
Telephone
01-858 8611

Hackney
Hackney Business Promotion Centre
1–11 Hoxton Street
London N1 6NL
Director
Dennis Statham
Telephone
01-739 7600 extn. 314
01-739 9606

Hackney
The Fashion Centre
165 Shoreditch High Street
London E1 6HU
Director
David Jones
Telephone
01-739 8857

Hammersmith & Fulham
Hammersmith & Fulham Business Resources Ltd
PO Box 501
Hammersmith Town Hall
King Street
London W6 9JU
Director
Tony Lloyd
Telephone
01-741 7248

Harrow
Harrow Enterprise Agency
Brush House
Rosslyn Crescent
Harrow
Middlesex
HA1 2SE
Director
Richard Robinson
Telephone
01-427 6188

Islington
Islington Small Business Counselling Service
202 Upper Street
Islington
London N1 1RQ
Manager
Norman Humphrey
Telephone
01-359 3924

Lambeth
Lambeth Business Advisory Service
Town Hall
Brixton Hill
London SW2
Director
Tom West
Telephone
01-274 7722

London
London Enterprise Agency (Lenta)
69 Cannon Street
London EC4 5AB
Director
Brian Wright MBE
Telephone
01-236 2676/7
01-248 4444

Park Royal (Ealing/Brent)
Park Royal Enterprise Trust
Waxlow Road
London NW10 7NU
Chairman
Jeff Goodman
Telephone
01-961 2717

Appendix B

Tower Hamlets
Tower Hamlets Centre for Small Businesses Ltd
99 Leman Street
London E1 8EY
Director
Barry Kennon
Telephone
01-481 0512

Vauxhall
Vauxhall Cross Amenity Trust
362 Kennington Lane
London SE11
Director
Alec Wrist
Telephone
01-597 1119

Wandsworth
Wandsworth Enterprise Development Agency
Unity House
56–60 Wandsworth High Street
London SW18 4LD
Director/General Manager
Denis Brookes
Telephone
01-870 2165

Wandsworth (Lenta)
Wandsworth Business Resource Service
140 Battersea Park Road
London SW11 4NB
Director
Keith Perks
Telephone
01-720 7053

Northern Ireland

Carrick Fergus
Enterprise Carrickfergus
c/o Courtaulds Ltd
72 Belfast Road
Carrickfergus
Co. Antrim
Director
Ron Wilson
Telephone
09603 68005

Northern Ireland
ARC — Northern Ireland
3 Botanic Avenue
Belfast
Manager
David Brown
Telephone
0232 234504
0232 231730

Wales

Deeside
Deeside Enterprise Trust Ltd
Park House
Deeside Industrial Park
Deeside
Clwyd
Director
Peter Summers MBE
Telephone
0244 815262

Neath
The Neath Partnership
c/o Thompson International
4 Stratford Place
London W1
Contact
J. A. Filmer-Bennett
Telephone
01-629 8111

Scotland

Ardrossan
Ardrossan Saltcoats Stevenston Enterprise Trust (ASSET)
21 Green Street
Ayrshire
Director
Douglas Martyn
Telephone
0294 602515

Kilmarnock
Kilmarnock Venture
Clydesdale Bank
30 The Foregate
Kilmarnock
Director
Willie McPhail
Telephone
0563 21140 (temporary)

153

APPENDIX C

INDEX OF ORGANISATIONS FOR WHOSE RETIRED EXECUTIVES REACH HAS SECURED SUITABLE MATCHES

Alcan
APV
Atlas Express Group
Bank of England
Barclays Bank
B A T Co
BBC
Beecham
Benn Bros
Boehringer Ingelheim
Bowater
BP
British Airways
British Aerospace
British Gas
British Steel
John Brown
Bunzl
Burmah Oil
Cable & Wireless
Cadbury Schweppes
Cape Industries
Chubb
Commercial Union
Consolidated Gold Fields
Costain
Courage

Courtaulds
Courts (Furnishers)
Deloitte Haskins & Sells
Delta
Electricity Council
Esso Petroleum
Evode
Fluor
GEC
Gestetner
Glaxo
Hawker Siddeley
Hogg Robinson
Hunting Group
IBM (United Kingdom)
ICI
IMI
Inchcape
International Computers
Johnson Matthey
Kodak
Mardon
Marks & Spencer
Midland Bank
Midlands Electricity Board
NAAFI
Nielsen

Overseas Containers
Pfizer
Phoenix Assurance
Pilkington
Plessey
P & O
Post Office
Powell Duffryn
Price Waterhouse
Ranks Hovis McDougall
Reckitt & Colman
Roche
Rolls-Royce
Royal Bank of Scotland
Sainsbury
Scottish & Newcastle Breweries
Scottish Gas
Standard Chartered Bank
Tarmac
Texaco
TI Group
Tootal
TSB
Turner & Newall
UAC International
Unigate
Waitrose

INDEX

Action Resource Centre, 38, 70
Additional Voluntary Contributions, 77
Allen, Cecilia, 39, 44, 70
Allman, Ralph, 62
Amnesty International Trust, 27
Armstrong, Jeff, 42
Aves Committee, 21

Barnardo's, 89
Barnett, Canon Samuel, 20
Bell, James, 128
Blume, Hilary, 126
Bolton Mountain Rescue Team, 109
Bone, Frances, 53
Bow Baths Community Centre, 17
British Executive Service Overseas (BESO), 113
British Steel Corporation, 41
Brixton United, 42
Brooks, Martin, 55
Broyd, Richard, 71
Burnbake Trust, 42
Burns, Peter, 128
Business in the Community, 40, 41, 70, 73

Cambridge House, 21
Cancer Research Campaign, 84
Cancer Research Fund, Imperial, 84
Charities Act 1960, 24
Charity Commissioners, 25, 26, 27
Charity Law Reform Committee, 30
Chick, Ronald, 48
Child Poverty Action Group, 24

Citizens' Advice Bureaux, 66
Community Health Councils, 66
Community Programme, 122
Companies Acts, 25
Community Projects Foundation, 49
Councils for Voluntary Service, 52, 64
Countrywide Workshops, 127
Coventry Cyrenians, 35
Craigmyle and Company, 127

DHSS, 12, 33, 39

Enterprise Agencies, 73
Enterprise Allowance Scheme, 74
Environment, Dept. of, 121
EXACT, 72

Factory and Public Health Acts, 19
Friends of the Earth, Scotland, 125

Gladstone, Francis, 26, 29
Glennerster, Howard, 23

Handy, Professor Charles, 32
Help the Aged, 106
Hill, Jenny, 33, 34, 35
Hinton, Nicholas, 22, 23, 31, 40, 49
Home Office, Voluntary Services Unit, 33, 53
Housing Corporation, 95

Industrial Revolution, 19
Industrial Society, 34

155

Ingram-Smith, Norman, 47
Inland Revenue, 28
Intaskill, 49
Intermediate Technology Development Group, 118

Jackson, Brian, 72

Leighton Buzzard Narrow Gauge Railway, 67
Levene, Robert, 60
Loan Guarantee Scheme, 74
Loudoun, Major-General Robert, 46

Manpower Services Commission, 11, 14, 39, 43, 74, 122
Marks and Spencer, 44
Mental Health Foundation, 46, 80

National Association of Community Relations Councils, 40
National Association of Victim Support Schemes, 46
National Council for Civil Liberties, 24
National Council for the Training of Journalists, 63
National Council for Voluntary Organisations, 22, 29, 32, 33, 34
National Extension College, 76
National Right to Read Campaign, 25
National Savings Income Bonds, 76
National Trust, 96
New Life Retirement Service, 75

O'Brien, Stephen, 40, 70, 73

Overseas Development Administration, 113, 118

Peterborough Society, 30
Piggott, Bill, 71
Pilkington, Sir Alastair, 43
Poor Law, 19
Poor Man's Lawyer service, 20
Project Fullemploy, 42
Public Voice Communications Ltd., 128

Rai, Dave, 47
Red Cross, 103
Reeves, Helen, 46
Rotary, 72
Royal National Lifeboat Institution, 87
Rural Community Councils, 66

Salvation Army, 92
Save the Children Fund, 100
Seebohm Report, 22
Settlements, 20; British Association of Settlements, 26; Lady Margaret Hall Settlement, 40
Shelter, 22, 25
Simmons, Joan, 45
Small Firms Service, 73
Social Action Centres, 26
St Martin-in-the-Fields, 47
Stubbings, Peter, 37
Success After Sixty, 71
Sykes, John, 53

Tank Museum, 78
Tax: capital, corporation, income, 27; development land tax, 28
Tickell, Tom, 76
Timbs, Tony, 74
Toynbee Hall, 20, 21
TUC, 23

Volunteer Bureaux, 52, 64
Volunteer Centre, 37, 64
Voluntary Service Overseas (VSO), 116

Welfare State, 21, 23
Wood-Grainger, Valerie, 127
Workshop, 6, 13

Youth Opportunities Programme, 11, 122
Youth Opportunities Scheme, 67
Youth Training Scheme, 11, 12, 42, 43, 122